Lilith: Queen of the Desert

Lilith: Queen of the Desert

by Anya Kless

Printed in the USA by Lulu Enterprises, Inc.

Published by Knickerbocker Circus Publishing
HTTP://WWW.KNICKERBOCKERCIRCUS.COM

Cover Design and Photograph by Katelan Foisy
www.katelanfoisy.com

ISBN 978-1-4507-2236-0

First Printing—July 2010

Acknowledgments

Many people encouraged me in this project and helped make it a reality.

First, I thank the talented contributors who made this project possible and gave it its heart's blood. Without you, I'd be standing on this path alone. I thank the countless others who came forward and sent small messages saying that they too know Lilith.

Thank you to the lovely and multi-talented Katelan Foisy, whose incredible, Lilith-inspired self-portrait serves as the cover of this volume. Stay classy.

Thank you to Tannin Schwarzstein who provided a wealth of resources on Lilith in print, online, and in cultural practice. It's all too rare to meet someone as equally devoted to the history, theory, and practice of spirituality.

Thank you to Galina Krasskova for introducing me to the devotional as a creative and religious form—as well as suggesting that I write this while it was still a choice and not a Job.

Thank you to Fire Tashlin for bringing Lilith to me in a new and unexpected light. I will never forget that day.

Finally, thank you to those who've paths I've crossed in the pagan and BDSM communities, as well as all those fighting all forms of social injustice on the front lines. You continue to model Lilith's timeless virtues: wisdom, freedom, authenticity, and absolute fearlessness.

For Lilith

Because I plunged into the unknown with only You at my side

Because I have known nothing as ferocious as my love for You

Because I was Yours first

Hail to You, Queen of the Desert

Table of Contents

Introduction: Hail Holy Queen

I am your daughter, teach me.
I am your sister, speak to me.
I am your priestess, embody me.

This was the first prayer I ever uttered to Lilith, even before I knew what it meant to be any of these things to Her. As She has for many others, Lilith entered my life when I found myself at a crossroads. I had just emerged—wounded and cynical—from a four and a half year relationship in which I'd felt the settled comforts of domesticity. Beneath the surface of that peaceful routine, however, ran currents of restlessness, repression, and betrayal on both sides. It was time to escape from the confines of my own flawed garden, to find my wings and fly into the unknown.

I did not immediately recognize Lilith when She came. Although I had been a practicing, eclectic pagan for several years, Lilith would be the first deity with whom I'd have an intense, personal relationship. One of my good friends is an initiate of Santeria, and after the breakup, I would accompany her to botanicas: crowded little spiritual supply stores that dot the Spanish neighborhoods of New York City. As I walked the aisles, I often felt inexplicably drawn to candles or baths for Santa Marta La Dominadora (the Snake Lady who dominates) or Oya (the Owl Lady who destroys). I bought them regularly for a few months, even though I had a lingering sense they weren't quite right. It was only after seeing a short chapter on Lilith in Tammy Sullivan's *Pagan Anger Magic* that I had my revelation. I found myself nodding vigorously at even the small amount of information on Her in that volume. *This* was My Lady. She had a modest altar in my bedroom the next day. Before I knew it, I was sitting naked on my wooden floor in a circle of red and black candles, feeling Her presence swirling around me like desert winds. And so we began.

Lilith challenged my assumptions about power, sexuality, sacrifice, and the sacred feminine. She spurred me to interrogate my own desires, those things I hid in my own dark places out of shame and fear. Shortly after meeting her, I became involved in BDSM, a world I had eyed with fascination and fear for many years. By choosing that path at my crossroads, I began a winding journey through the abject places of submission and slavery, as well as the heady rush of dominance and mastery. It was a dizzying path of painful self-discovery, new responsibilities, and, in short, an incredible education.

Across the years, Lilith has trained and shaped me as a student, a devotee, and a priestess. She taught me what it is to work for a deity, to worship a deity, to speak with a deity, and to love a deity. Her lessons have laid the foundations for relationships I would have with later deities, which I am quite sure would have been far more jarring and difficult had She not prepared the way. I owe Her quite a bit, and this devotional is one opportunity to give my services to Her.

When I asked Lilith what She wanted for this project, She gave two clear messages. First, *"this is not an academic text."* As a former academic who recently finished doctoral work, this immediately took me out of my comfort zone. I knew at that point that any research I did for this devotional would be secondary—and in service to a larger goal.

Part I of this project serves as my compromise with Lilith on this front. While not strictly academic—in the sense of engaging in analytical or comparative work—it gives a basic overview of "Lilith in History" for those unfamiliar with Her legacy. In the last 30 years, a handful of historians and scholars have uncovered and compiled references to Lilith's origins, stories, mythology, and cultural impact in ancient texts. Most volumes give only a short entry on Lilith as an interesting anomaly, but Patai's *The Hebrew Goddess* provides perhaps the lengthiest, most comprehensive account of Lilith, drawing upon a wealthy of primary sources from many cultures and communities. Besides information on early writings, this section examines the evolution of perceptions and representations of Lilith in the modern age. It briefly looks at how various twentieth and twenty-first century groups have called upon Lilith, identified with Her, and incorporated Her into their own goals and agendas. Anyone looking for a more academic approach to Lilith should see the "Further Reading" list at the end of this volume.

If not an academic study, what then is the point of this volume? Lilith's second message gave this instruction: *"speak of me as you know me."* While Lilith has often been discussed as a cultural archetype, a relic, and a myth, She is rarely approached as a real and vital being. As far as I know, She has never had a full-length project on Her intimate yet overpowering presence in the lives of individual people living now. This project aims takes a small step towards filling that void.

In Part II of this book, you'll find an introduction to working with Lilith on a personal basis. This section begins with a frank discussion of the potential dangers of allowing Lilith into your life. After the disclaimers, it gives initial suggestions as to correspondences, offerings, and altars. I've also included information about the faces of Lilith most often encountered by contemporary practitioners and why you might want to invite in a certain aspect of Her. At the end of this section, there is a short ritual (which can be altered and customized as needed) to honor Lilith and begin a relationship with Her...if She hasn't initiated one with you already.

Part III of this project appeared rather unexpectedly. As I began outlining this book, I looked through journals in which I'd recorded my communications from Her. On one page, I found a request She had made for a set of prayers on seven specific needs. I had forgotten about the entry but realized that if I were to ever write the prayers, now would be the time. As I composed them, I was surprised to see them take shape as Songs, in the vein of The Songs of Solomon (whom some speculate may have been one of Her consorts). I've written and included them in the order they were presented to me, even if it seemed contrary to my logic. In this order they have their own logic: Hers. They are here not as holy words to be memorized and recited by rote, although new and seasoned folk should feel free to use them. I see them as seeds— points of departure for meditations on Lilith, meditations on our own needs, and opening a line of conversation with Her.

Part IV stands as the heart of this book, containing invocations, prayers, poems, songs, and short reflections from those who honor Lilith, know Her, and love Her. I have organized this section by some the many faces of Lilith as experienced by Her people. I was fortunate to receive submissions that covered a wide range of perspectives and was intrigued by the common threads that connected them. Of course, this sampling is not exhaustive and should not be seen as a definitive outline of Her possibilities.

Finally, I end this volume with a short message in Lilith's own words and a bibliography for further reading. For those looking for more specialized accounts of Lilith in religious, cultural, historical, astrological, and psychological contexts, this is the place to begin.

Part I: Lilith in History

Who is Lilith?

Lilith is a figure of multiplicity and contradiction. Her name currently serves as the title of a progressive, Jewish women's magazine, hundreds of years after their ancestors warded their children against her murderous clutches. Asteroids and astrological phenomena bear her name. Her stories can be found in a number of ancient religious, folk, and mystical texts, including Sumerian, Babylonian, Hebraic, Zoharian, and Kabbalistic sources. She has multiple origins, multiple forms, and multiple consorts. There is even debate about what Lilith is—Goddess? Demon? Wind Spirit? Vampire? Cultural Force? First Woman? Archetype of the Dark Feminine? Is Lilith a Female? Hermaphrodite? Androgyne? Is she a sexy seductress or a hairy, indeterminate figure with the lower body of a goat?

Unlike many figures, Lilith lacks a single narrative. As someone who loves Lilith, I look across the varied terrain of our attempt to know Her and see a rich history. In the brief account below, I have given some foundational information about how Lilith has appeared in cultures across time. A complete knowledge of the many communities, fields, and movements that have claimed Her is not necessary for working with Lilith, but it can enrich our understanding of where She has been and where She might be going. For an in-depth study, please seek out the works in the annotated bibliography at the end of this volume.

Earliest Traces

The multiplicity of Lilith's origins and cultural influences becomes apparent even in seeking the etymology of Her name. In Sumerian writings, Lilith or "Lillake" seems descended from a class of demons called "Lillu" or "Lili," meaning "storm demon" or " wind demon." There is also the Babylonian-Assyrian word "lilitu," one of a triad mentioned in Babylonian spells, meaning female demon or wind-spirit. According to popular Hebrew etymology, "Lilith'" stems from LYL, "layil" or night; while Babylonian and Sumerian sources depict Her as a succubus or demoness, in Hebraic and Arabian folklore She more often appears as a hairy night-monster.[1] Scholars have made connections between Lilith and the Babylonian goddess Lamashtû, the figure of Karina in Arabic literature, as well as the vampiric Lamia in ancient Greek writings.[2] More recently, M. Kelley Hunter has made the connection between Lilith's name and the lily, which "grows out of dark, rank, decaying earth, and represents spiritual unfolding and the blossoming of the heart of wisdom."[3]

Sumerian and Babylonian

The earliest surviving written references to Lilith—or what some have called Lilith—come from Sumeria. The Sumerian king list, dating from ca. 2400 B.C.E, states that the father of the epic hero Gilgamesh was in fact "Lillu," a demon. In *Gilgamesh and the*

1 Patai 222.

2 Hurwitz 36.

3 Hunter 15.

Huluppu Tree, the great Sumerian epic found on a tablet dating from 2000 B.C.E., a creature named "Lillake" resides within a Huluppu (willow) tree at the bank of the Euphrates, the cradle of civilization. "Lillake," whom many see as Lilith Herself, shares the tree with a dragon at the base and a large bird at the crown. The tree is tended to by Anath, whom many read as the Goddess Inanna. According to the epic, this tree has stood since the dawn of creation. As part of his heroic journey, Gilgamesh, representing a new world order, slays the dragon with an axe, causing the bird to fly away and "Lillake" to flee into the desert.[4]

The Huluppu Tree has been seen as a parallel to the Tree of Knowledge in the Hebraic creation story, and, as we'll see below, Lilith has also figured prominently in depictions of that Tree. According to M. Kelley Hunter, "the serpent represents the chthonic wisdom of earth, oracular powers, and the *kundalini*, the subtle life force that awakens consciousness as it courses up the tree of the spinal cord. Winding in the roots of the tree, the serpent also grounds the energy into the earth."[5]

In the Gilgamesh story, Lilith appears as the foe of Inanna, taking residence in a tree the young goddess had hoped to use as a throne and marriage bed. In another Sumerian text, however, Inanna sends the beautiful and seductive "Lilitu" into the streets and fields to lead men astray. A nearly identical tale exists in a Babylonian text, which lists Lilith as a sacred prostitute of Ishtar—

---

4 Patai 222.

5 Hunter 5.

who corresponds to the Sumerian Inanna. Thus, Lilith has been called both the "Hand of Ishtar" and the "Hand of Inanna."[6] In the UPG of some modern day practitioners, Lilith has spoken of the Whore of Babylon, Baphomet, and a few other "old world" figures as Her siblings, although the literal or metaphorical way in which She conceives of family relations remains somewhat hazy.[7]

One of the most controversial pieces of Lilith archeology is the Burney Relief, a Babylonian terracotta relief dated to around 2000 B.C.E. and now held in the British Museum. The now popular image shows a nude woman with wings and a bird's taloned feet. She wears a hat composed of four pairs of horns and holds in each upraised hand a combined ring and rod (similar to an Egyptian amulet). She stands on two reclining lions and is flanked by owls. Although this image is routinely identified as (and sold in reproduction as) a representation of Lilith, scholars disagree on the identity of the figure depicted as Inanna/Ishtar, Ereshkigal, Lilith, or another feminine figure who may have been lost to history all together.[8]

Jewish and Christian

According to Jewish folklorist Howard Schwartz, "among the

---

6 Hurwitz 58.

7 UPG stands for "Unverified Personal Gnosis." It refers to information devotees have gleaned from personal encounters with deities that may not be verifiable through known textual evidence. If several practitioners have been given the same information, it becomes PCPG ("peer-corroborated personal gnosis") or SPG ("shared personal gnosis").

8 Personally, I do not associate this image with Lilith, although I've found that She does share certain qualities with it. Despite the lack of scholarly evidence, I do not wish to dismiss others' associations with it, only to make readers aware of the questions surrounding the image.

legends with biblical origins and rabbinic and folk elaborations, none had a greater influence than that of Lilith. It is not an exaggeration to say that much of the demonic realm in Jewish folklore grew out of this multifaceted legend, which came into being as a commentary on one passage of the Bible, '*Male and Female He created them*' (Gen. 1:27)."[9] The line of Genesis Schwartz cites has troubled biblical scholars for centuries because there are in fact two creation stories. In Genesis I, God seemingly creates man and woman simultaneously, while in the more famous and elaborate creation story in Genesis 2, Yahweh creates Eve from Adam's rib after man cannot find companionship with animals alone. Most modern biblical scholars see this discrepancy as evidence of multiple authorship by multiple communities across multiple centuries (hence the use of different names for 'God' in different sections, including "Yahweh" and "Elohim").[10] They have come to see the Hebrew Bible (or for Christians, the Old Testament) as a patchwork anthology of cultural and religious writings. Early rabbis, however, who interpreted the text for their communities, worked from the belief that the Pentateuch (first five books of the Bible) had been dictated directly to Moses from their god. Because of this, every word of the Bible must be literally true. So why two creation stories?

The solution to the contradiction first appeared in *The Alphabet*

---

9 Schwartz 5.

10 To differentiate the Judeo-Christian god from other gods, this text will use the name "Yahweh" to refer to him.

of Ben Sira, written in the eleventh century in Persia or Arabia.[11] The author of the text claimed that the first passage referred to the creation of Adam and his first wife, Lilith, while the second referred to the creation of Eve. Adam and Lilith quarreled endlessly, in later adaptations because Lilith refused to lie beneath Adam during intercourse. She refuses the traditional submissive role with Her husband, insisting instead on equality. Frustrated, Lilith pronounces the secret name of Yahweh, sprouts wings, and flies out of the Garden of Eden to the shores of the Red Sea. She takes up residence in a desert cave, taking demons as Her lovers and giving birth the world's supply of demons. Lonely and emasculated, Adam complains to Yahweh, who sends the angels Snvi, Snsvi, and Smnglof to command Lilith to return. When she refuses, the angels kill one hundred of Her demon children daily. Lilith, however, remained unmoved.

Because of the satirical nature of *The Alphabet of Ben Sira,* scholars have questioned the author's seriousness. Regardless of its original intent, however, the connection between Lilith and the first Eve struck a chord with Jewish folk imagination, and it is now an inexorable part of those traditions. As in Sumerian and Babylonian legends dating from around 3,500 B.C.E., Lilith becomes a winged female demon who kills infants and endangers women in childbirth. In this role, she is one of several *mazakim* or "harmful spirits" known from incantation formulas preserved in Assyrian, Hebrew, and Canaanite inscriptions intended to protect against them.

---

11 Schwartz 5.

According to *The Alphabet,* Lilith proclaims that she had been created to snatch the souls of infants, and she vowed that only if confronted with an amulet bearing the names of the three angels (Snvi, Snsvi, and Smnglof) would she do no harm.[12] In late Roman and early medieval Judaism, Lilith's image frequently appears on magical bowls, countered by the written names of the three angels. Aramaic incantation texts in 600 C.E. Babylonia, those from a Jewish colony at Nippur, and those in Persia have all shared wards against Lilith.[13]

In medieval and renaissance art, Lilith's role in Christian folklore can also been seen. While in Jewish lore Lilith escapes the Garden, in Christian lore She returns in the guise of the serpent that tempts Eve. Several depictions of the temptation scenes contain an odd central image: a half-woman, half-serpent hanging in the Tree of Knowledge, beckoning to Eve. As Hunter notes, the north side West Portal of the Virgin of Notre Dame Cathedral and Michelangelo's famous ceiling in the Sistine Chapel both feature this hybrid figure, whom she identifies as Lilith, handing Eve the apple.[14]

Despite Lilith's official status as a figure of evil, immorality, and destruction, the lingering fascination with Her across cultures seems rooted in more than just fear and revulsion. There is something seductive about Lilith for members of both sexes. She stands as the

---

12 Schwartz 5.

13 Patai 228.

14 Hunter 7.

dark teacher. Lilith as the succubus serves as a scapegoat for men's "nocturnal emissions" and sexual fantasies. In several Jewish folktales she tutors rogue rabbis "in the ways of black magic."[15] In rethinking the magic bowls that bear Her image or name, they almost seem to cast Lilith Herself as a ward against evil (or at least as an evil that can be reasoned with and appeased). Even tales that seem to portray Her as a force of destruction offer alternative models of femininity and perhaps a critique of the patriarchal structures of Jewish culture. In the tale "Lilith's Cave," Lilith comes through an old mirror to possess the daughter of the house through her eyes. The tale states:

> For every mirror is a gateway to the Other World and leads directly to Lilith's Cave. That is the cave Lilith went to when she abandoned Adam and the Garden of Eden for all time, the cave where she sported with her demon lovers....That is why it is said that Lilith makes her home in every mirror.[16]

Once inside the daughter, Lilith drives her to engage in behavior that ruins her reputation: she stays out all night and has countless sexual partners. The father becomes so ashamed and furious that he curses his daughter, transforming her into a bat. As punishment for expressing her newly found sexuality, she will flit from man to man in the night forever.

Presumably, the tale serves to warn daughters against vanity (staring into a mirror) and promiscuity. It is possible, however, to see an alternative reading just below the surface. Notably, Lilith only

---

15 Schwartz 3.

16 "Lilith's Cave" (120-1). Howard Schwartz, *Lilith's Cave.*

appears after the mother of the house has died, having inhaled a feather from a pillow. Perhaps the settled life of a housewife does not hold much reward for the young girl either. Better to haunt the night than choke on domesticity.

Kabbalah

Considering Her associations with forbidden knowledge and magic, it is not surprising that Lilith's mythos is taken up again in Spanish Kabbalistic writings during the 13th century. She gained even more origin stories, stemming from even more re-readings of Genesis. In one version, Lilith appears on the fifth day of creation as a creature who swarms the waters. In another, She is created by 'God' out of "impure earth" while Adam is created from sacred ground. In yet another, Her soul is called up to join Adam's from "the Great Abyss."[17] In some versions, She is even considered "a divine entity" that emerged "out of the power aspect of God (the *Gevurah* or *Din*)."[18] In the mystical system of Kabbalah—yet another Tree of Life with which Lilith is associated—*Gevurah* represents Severity while Din represents Judgment. In this aspect, Lilith acts as the force which punishes the wicked and judges humanity.

In Kabbalistic writings, Lilith is sometimes split into Lilith the Younger and Lilith the Elder. Younger Lilith acts as the wife of Ashmodai/Asmodeus, whom Judeo-Christian mystics have

17 Patai 230.

18 Patai 230.

identified as the King of Demons or King of the Nine Hells. In 1589, Peter Binsfield's classifications of demons assigned each of the major demons with one of the seven deadly sins. Asmodeus rules lust, making him a fitting partner for the dark or forbidden sexuality Lilith traditionally represents. Lilith the Elder, alternately, is cast as the wife of Samael. In Talmudic and post-Talmudic Jewish lore, Samael appears as an archangel and a fallen angel, as well as the Angel of Death. Paradoxically, he is considered both good and evil, a seducer, destroyer, and guardian.[19] In *The Hebrew Goddess,* Patai cites a Zoharic myth in which "out of the dregs of wine, there emerged an intertwined shoot which comprises both male and female. They are red like the rose, and they spread out into several sides and paths. The male is called Samael, and his female [Lilith] is always contained in him....The female of Samael is called Serpent, Woman of Harlotry, End of All Flesh, End of Days."[20] Lilith and Samael together represent the fecundity of androgyny and ambiguity. They are two creatures in one flesh, siblings who are lovers, the beginning and the end.

In addition to Her demonic/angelic consorts, Lilith also becomes the consort of Yahweh after the destruction of the Temple and the exile of the people of Israel.[21] In the traditional hierarchy, the pair of Yahweh and the Shekhina (the feminine force or dwelling place of Yahweh) above is mirrored by Samael and Lilith below. After the loss of the Temple, however, the Shekhina

---

19 Patai 247.

20 Patai 230-1.

21 Patai 250.

descends to follow her wandering flock, and Lilith, her handmaiden, ascends to take her place. Although in Jewish and Kabbalistic lore this transition is seen as a loss of perfection and entrance into a state of "fallenness", it also suggests that, like his people, Yahweh possesses a lingering desire for Lilith. Some modern feminist and pagan writers have attempted to put forward Lilith and the Shekhina as goddesses actively worshipped covertly by ancient Jewish communities. For example, Barbara Koltuv notes that "both Lilith and the Shekhina represent the rejected Goddess's quality of prophetic inner knowledge."[22] Historically, however, there is no evidence that Jewish communities worshipped any feminine figure (just as there now seems to be little evidence of a pre-patriarchal, goddess worshipping era in Western Europe). Modern practitioners may forge their own way here.

Astrology

Several astronomical entities have been named Lilith, including an asteroid, a star, a shadow moon (called the Dark Moon), and a vortex in the Earth-Moon system (the Black Moon). Contemporary astrologers can use the placement of these entities in one's chart to gain insight into personal qualities and potential paths. The best collection of information on Lilith in astrological terms is M. Kelley Hunter's book, *Living Lilith: Four Dimensions of the Cosmic Feminine*. In it, she explores the characteristics and influences of each Lilith-

---

22 Koltuv 7.

26

related form, in addition to giving a formula for finding the various "Liliths" in your own chart.

Each of the four astrological appearances of Lilith hold pieces of her earlier mythologies. For example, Hunter notes how Black Moon Lilith "faces us with a stark, still void, inherently uncomfortable, even terrifying."[23] Lilith the star, found in the constellation Perseus, is officially named Algol, the "demon" star. Hunter also notes that it was sometimes called Lilith by the Hebrews but does not give a source for this information. Because of its location in Perseus, Hunter links Lilith with the Greek figure Medusa, whose severed, snake-covered head Perseus holds in the constellation. She notes, "Algol marks the paralyzing eye of Medusa, with the look that turns one to stone."[24] It should also be noted that the field of studying pain is known as Algolology.

Psychology

During the nineteenth century, Western European art and literature became obsessed with the monstrous images of femininity.[25] In 1868, Dante Gabriel Rossetti painted "Lady Lilith" with a cruel, twisted smile. It is not surprising, therefore, that the burgeoning fields of psychology and psychoanalysis tried to make sense of Lilith at the end of the century. Usually She represented

---

23 Hunter 24.

24 Hunter 25.

25 Bram Dijkstra has written twice on this in *Idols of Perversity: Fantasies of Feminine Evil in Fin-de-siècle Culture* (1986); and *Evil Sisters: The Threat of Female Sexuality and the Cult of Manhood* (1996).

the feminine, dark side of the self, which men both feared and desired. Carl Jung used Lilith as his prime expression of the *anima* in men, the suppressed feminine force within.[26]

Failure to embrace Lilith, whether as the anima or shadow self, meant that one could not be psychologically whole. Adherents of this philosophy often point to Adam's failure to accept Lilith as an equal as the first struggle between the incomplete ego and the fulness of the "Deeper Self." As Koltuv notes, "while we have repeatedly seen that there is a psychological need to know and integrate Lilith as both the personal and collective feminine shadow, the primary and traditional patriarchal model for dealing with her has been to suppress or cast her out."[27] In this light, perhaps rather than getting in touch with our inner child, we all need to get in touch with our inner Lilith.

Feminism

Lilith's refusal to lie beneath Adam, according to the tale told in the *Alphabet of Ben Sira*, has made Her a modern feminist icon. She has become a symbol of resistance to patriarchal authority, female independence, and freedom from male oppression at any cost. Ironically, She has been particularly embraced by Jewish feminists (hence the magazine for progressive Jewish women entitled *Lilith*), despite Her traditional cultural role as a killer of Jewish infants.

---

26 For a reading of Lilith from a Jungian perspective, the best example is Hurwitz, one of Jung's disciples. See the "Further Reading" list.

27 Koltuv 91.

In feminism's reading, Lilith's "bad reputation" stems from Her threat to male authority, the traditional writers of history. Images of Her as a demon or dangerous force are chalked up to scare tactics designed to keep women in place. Put simply, Lilith is what happens when women disobey. She personifies the full range of female sexuality—beyond fertility—and its potential power.

Neo-Paganism

Following Jungian psychology and feminism, some neo-pagan groups and writers have claimed Lilith as an empowering force. With the rise of Dianic Traditions or Goddess Spirituality, Lilith became an emblem of the sacred feminine that had been rejected and slandered by patriarchal, monotheistic forces. Other neo-pagans of Jewish ancestry have identified Lilith as an ancient goddess alongside the Shekhina, including Starhawk and Jennifer Hunter (author of *Mythical Judaism*).[28] More generally, Lilith has found Her way onto the roster of "dark" goddesses, an eclectic list that often includes figures like Hecate, Kali, Ereshkigal, the Morrigan, and Sekhmet.

Satanism

Satanists hail Lilith variously as the Bride of Satan, Satan's daughter, the Queen of Hell (or Princess of Hell, if they're envisioning a younger, sexier figure), the Mother of All Demons,

---

28 Many thanks to Tannin Schwartzstein for this information. She also noted that Canaanite Pagans she has met, which strong Jewish backgrounds, have not adopted Lilith.

the sister of Cain, and/or the sister of Lucifer. Gleaning information from Kabbalist texts, some recognize Her as the bride of Samael, called the Dark Angel or Angel of Death. Most of Satanic/Luciferian lore seems to be cobbled together from older mythologies, sometimes with confusing and conflicting results. (For example, many Satanic amulets for sale claiming to feature Lilith and Samael instead show an image of the goat-headed Baphomet). Theistic Satanist Geifodd ap Pwyll, who has written of Lilith online, does make one interesting claim about Lilith's change in status in the modern age: "Perhaps Lilith the demoness became Lilith the goddess in today's world because *today's world is more agreeable with Her nature* than the ancient one was."[29]

Vampirism

In a Marvel comic book published in 1974, *Giant-Size Chillers featuring Curse of Dracula* #1, Lilith appeared as the daughter of Dracula. Since then, She has had a place in vampire lore either as the first and most powerful vampire or their queen. The more recent rise of Sanguinarian vampirism as a subculture, lifestyle, and identity has brought a new community to Lilith. Source materials in this community include the roleplaying game *Vampire: the Masquerade* and the writings of Viola Johnson, also a pioneer of the BDSM community. For more information on Lilith from a Sanguinarian perspective, read Raven Orthaevelve's essay "Lilith's Service" on page 106.

---

29 "There's something about Lilith," at http://theisticsatanism.com/geifodd /lilith.html

Transgender

As far as I know, Raven Kaldera's *Hermaphrodeities* was the first text to identify Lilith as a transgender icon, even if the qualities that make Her a candidate for this role can be found in much older stories and writings (see his essay on Lilith's role in his own transition on page 85). In my own community, I know of several people who have been claimed by Lilith either before or during an exploration or transition in their gender. Besides aspects of Her physical appearance that challenge traditional gender roles, several of Lilith's stories involve hermaphroditic origins. She springs to life as both Adam and Samael's other half, literally two beings in one body. Sam's

Part II: Meeting Lilith

Disclaimers and Dangers

Inviting any deity into your life carries inevitable consequences, not all of them easy or pleasant. Depending on the extent of your relationship with said deity, you may go in with little control of what may occur or be asked of you. While I'm not one to believe that this should deter potential devotees, I do think people should go into a relationship with any deity with their eyes open. Gods are not vending machines, ready to provide whatever your heart desires in exchange for a nicely carved candle. Rather than giving us what *we want,* they more often bring the change we do not yet realize *we need.* Even if we do not immediately recognize it as such, this is a huge gift.

As your relationship unfolds, you will be surprised and taken off your guard as a matter of course. The following paragraphs, however, establish a rudimentary primer to what those pursuing (or being pursued by) Lilith may reasonably expect.

While some deities may operate in the gray area of ethics, Lilith is not one of those. She has a very clear understanding of Right and Wrong. It is very possible, however, that Her code of ethics will not match your own. Additionally, any violation of that code—by you or those in your life—may be dealt with brutally (we're talking things like cancer and miscarriages, both of which I've seen Her bring). If Lilith determines that such things are deserved or the best possible outcome, She will not hesitate to serve as the Bringer of

Justice. She has little tolerance for injustice, particularly against women or those not in traditional positions of power.

Does this mean that Lilith will eagerly smite your enemies while you sit back and enjoy? Hardly. It is far more likely that She will push you to remedy the situation yourself. She can be a destructive force, particularly if She believes something in your life is unhealthy or unproductive. Lilith smashes those toxic things in our lives that we may be unable (or unwilling) to get rid of ourselves: jobs, partners, friends, living situations, life choices (personally, I have lost *all* of these due to Lilith's influence). This is Her gift, and it can be incredibly valuable.

Lilith is excellent at showing you your path, but She does this by destroying all that is *not* your path. In this way, She reminds me of The Tower card in tarot: creative destruction, forcing us to break out of constricting forms that no longer serve us. Like the snake, one of Her emblems, Lilith is a catalyst for shedding old skin. It can be terrifying to let go of the familiar, but I can say with certainty that if Lilith takes something away, you are better off without it. Trust Her on this.

One last disclaimer: Lilith is a very "tit for tat" entity. She operates on a system of fair, equal exchange. If you ask Her for favors without giving payment, you won't get far with Her. You may even irritate Her and be taught a lesson about etiquette. She will keep you honest about the proportion of your offerings. If she gives a large "blessing" and you absentmindedly light Her a candle, that won't cut it. This does not mean that Lilith requires expensive gifts or basins of your own blood—it is more likely she will require your time and energy. One of the best offerings to Lilith is to devote an entire evening to honoring and being open to Her presence, whether in dancing, chanting, or silent meditation.

Lilith's Lessons

Lilith can be a powerful teacher—wise, patient, and generous with Her attention. It's impossible to predict what lessons She will bring into any individual life, but the list below comprises the most common. Not surprisingly, all of these trials appear somewhere in Her *mythos,* lessons She herself has had to master. If you find yourself struggling in one or more of these realms, approach Her humbly and honestly to ask for aid. If these issues have appeared unexpectedly—and in a way that they can no longer be ignored— you can read it as Her own signature across your life.

Self-knowledge

"Know thyself," is a centuries old maxim, to the point that it's become almost cliché. But what does it really mean, and how can we tell if we *do* know ourselves? Often it's easier to tell when we don't know ourselves. How in touch are we with our own desires? It can be tempting to treat life like a conveyor belt: leading us through the standard milestones of school, work, marriage, kids, the white picket fence. Lilith causes us to ask what we truly want rather than what we feel we *should* want—or what society tells us we should want.

When people don't want to know themselves, they often spend as little time with themselves as possible. They may busy themselves with a packed social calendar or work. They may be inseparable from their partner, molding their own life around another's. Even if they spend most of their time alone, they may live vicariously through TV or the internet. If you cannot spend quiet time with yourself comfortably, chances are you don't *want* to know yourself. Lilith will nudge you to determine why this is. What do you fear or loathe about yourself? Can you stand before a mirror, literally and figuratively naked of all that conceals you?

Authenticity

In any quest for self-knowledge, we will inevitably come across some parts of ourselves we deem too ugly to ever see the light of day. It's the moment of turning over a rock and seeing insects swarm up from underneath. These may be things we need to face and work to release: vanity, jealousy, greed, obsession. Some things we uncover, however, may be essential pieces of our identity— pieces that society has deemed too scary, too depraved, or just taboo. It is these pieces that Lilith will not allow us to hide or throw away.

Lilith demands that we own the outcast parts of ourselves. It may not be enough that we acknowledge them; Lilith may push us to live them, particularly if it involves our gender or sexuality. Lilith has little tolerance for things repressed or closeted, those things we fantasize about but deem impossible. Although she will probably not demand that you tell your office about your BDSM adventures, she will demand that you at least *have* those adventures. We must look over the walls of the garden we've constructed for ourselves, aware of the alternatives.

Transformation

In order to live with authenticity, to break out of the limits others have imposed on us (or that we've imposed on ourselves), we will need to shed our old skin. Keep in mind one of Lilith's most powerful symbol is the snake. Some things must be discarded for others to be gained. If we are not willing to let go of that which no longer serves us, we will remain paralyzed. We must undergo a process of death and rebirth to come into the full potentiality of our nascent selfhood.

Letting go of the familiar, even if it's currently making us miserable, can be exceptionally difficult and painful. It is not surprising that Lilith often appears when we stand on the cusp of transformation. For most, we need Lilith's destructive hand to topple some of our towers for us—or at least to remind us, "if you don't, I will." We must face the fear of losing everything—including ourselves—to known true freedom.

Despair

Lilith loses many things in Her stories: paradise, power, partners, and countless children. Many of those who communicate with Her share the sense that She has been betrayed, treated unjustly, and slandered for the betterment of the dominant social order. She is kin to those who find themselves misunderstood, demonized, and scapegoated due to fear and prejudice. Lilith knows desolation and despair. She is the patron of the lost and the forgotten, the outcast and the outlaw, the suicidal and the self-loather.

The first time I felt Lilith's despair during a solo ritual for Her I was caught off guard. I had worked with Her for years and had never held this part of Her before. It wracked my body with sobs to feel the thwarted desire twined with anger. Like all parts of Lilith, Her despair can be ferocious and consuming. Approaching Her in this state, however, we can find an outlet for immense pain and isolation. Be warned that Lilith will not look kindly on those who wallow melodramatically or take refuge in victimhood. For those in earnest need, however, She can serve as an ally even here, in the pit of utter darkness.

Anger

Anger can be one of the most difficult emotions to process in a healthy manner. It is all too easy to either let it explode or swallow it, letting it control us in either mode. Either it blows up in our face or slowly eats away at us from within. If not handled properly, it can do a lot of damage. As a deity associated with righteous anger, Lilith can be an excellent teacher in this realm.

When I was a girl, my mother told me that if someone bothered me or bullied me, I should simply ignore them. Because of this, I learned to repress my anger towards others. After Lilith came into my life, however, I was no longer allowed to get away with this. On one occasion, a colleague said something insulting to me, and I let it go for the sake of keeping the peace. That night when I got into bed, I felt like I had a burning coal in my chest. I literally burned with anger and couldn't sleep for two days. Finally I wrote the person an email, firmly telling them that they'd angered me and why. Sometimes Lilith can be even more dramatic. One night, a guest arrived at my home seven hours late because she had badly mismanaged her time. I was furious but attempted to be polite and sympathetic. After only a few minutes of social pleasantry, my wine glass flew out of my hand and shattered on the floor, splashing red liquid and tiny shards everywhere. It was a sign to get rid of the facade and be sincere, even if it meant "not being nice". Lilith gives us permission to own our anger—not to bully others but in order to make ourselves heard.

Power

Like anger, power can be a dirty word. Because of the way it has traditionally been used and abused, it may be hard to conceptualize power without envisioning power over someone else. For those of us who work with deities, it can be tempting to place our lives completely in their hands and go on autopilot. Conversely, it can be tempting to see magical work as a gateway to unlimited power with no consequences or responsibilities.

Lilith will demand that you take back the reigns in your life. While some things may lie outside of your control, you may be surprised at how many choices you have. Consider how effectively you use the power you have—how well do you wield it? Do you take responsibility for your actions? Do you give your power away to others in exchange for complacency and dependence? Do you abuse your power to feed your own ego?

Correspondences

Below I've listed some of the most popular associations devotees seem to have with Lilith. This is by no means an exhaustive list or set of rigid guidelines, merely a starting place.

Colors: black, red, gold, bronze, the color of dust or sand, the colors of decomposing or rotting things

Animals: snakes, owls, bats, lions, traditionally "unclean" or "vermin" animals, black or red creatures

Stones and metals: onyx, bloodstone, agate, ruby, garnet, gold, bronze, black pearl, hematite, apache tear, smokey quartz, jet

Organic materials: incense, sulfur, snake skin, feathers, bone, sand, dirt, ash, charcoal, anything left to decompose on Her altar

Times: Fridays, nighttime, midnight, the dark moon, eclipses

Lilith and the Elements

Lilith is one of the few deities I've encountered that I can associate with each of the four elements. Considering Her many lessons and the richness of Her history, this is not surprising. The purpose of your work with Her may dictate the aspect of Lilith you invoke, the form of your offering, and the tools you use to accomplish your work. See the "Offerings" section below for more detail on what to give.

Air

In earliest record, Lilith appears as a wind demon, unsettling the order of civilization. Taking on the energies and form of air, Lilith is the sudden breeze that shoves us on the street or turns our umbrella inside out. It's a sign to pay attention—or that some necessary work has been neglected. She may come as a winged messenger, a harbinger of change and new ideas. Like Her animal the owl, She brings gifts of wisdom, insight, and discernment, if we are wise enough to understand. As the saying goes, wisdom is a gift for the wise. Incense, rattles, bells, or hand cymbals (those traditional to belly dancing) make appropriate offerings.

Fire

In Her fiery face, Lilith consumes and destroys. Like roaring flames, She feeds off that which we cast off, the garbage and waste of our lives. Out of this sacrifice, however, emerges a new form. Her hunger can leave a place of barrenness, like the landscape after a forest fire or the scorched earth of a desert. When we've cluttered our lives with unnecessary things, persons, or concerns, however, the wide, empty space of smoldering ash can revitalize us. Lilith as fire brings a new beginning: She is the RESET button. While She will not "fix" all our problems, She will assist us in tackling them. Red or black candles are best here, particularly those you've carved with Her name or symbols. Charcoal, ash, or sand will also serve.

Earth

Quite simply, Lilith's tie to earth is the body. Lilith teaches us to live authentically within our bodies, whatever their shape, appearance, or functionality. By calling upon Lilith as a creature of earth, we face those things society deems "impure" or "unclean" about our bodies. We celebrate the power our bodies can produce through physical labor, sexual acts, and artistic expression. Keep in mind, however, that earthy Lilith can also bring physical ordeals, particularly those meant to transform, purge, or cleanse our bodies. Earth offerings include dancing, sex in all its forms, animal parts (bones, skin, feathers), tattoos in Her honor, jewelry, and nakedness itself.

Water

Lilith as water represents the unknown: the dark water that conceals what lies beneath the surface. She lurks in the shadows of our unconscious with the other monsters that hide there, waiting to come to the surface. Watery Lilith holds our secrets, the things we tell no one, and will press us to out them or process them. Or both. She brings murkiness, ambiguity, and intuition, particularly if we've become too wedded to seeing the world through a lens of strict rationality and reason. She teaches that things are seldom what they appear to be and that snap judgments or labels rarely serve us. Some of Lilith's favorite offerings fall under this category, including red wine, blood, and sexual fluids (see below). Tears, however, may also be required, as well as spoken or written confessions.

Offerings

I tend to make offerings to Lilith on Friday evenings. This is the day I most associate with Her, although if I feel Her presence around, I will approach Her regardless of the day. Go to Her at night in a candlelit room. The darker Her space, the better. In Lilith's case, darkness does not represent evil—it is the darkness of the shadow, the hidden, the unknown. By walking into Her darkness, we show a willingness to leave the trappings of civility behind and encounter Her on Her turf, whether in the desert, cave, gnarled tree, or void.

In Tammy Sullivan's *Pagan Anger Magic,* she notes that Lilith's three favorite offerings are blood, red wine, and sexual fluids. In my years of practice, I have found this to be true. On first glance this can be an intimidating list, conjuring images of frenzied orgies or basins of spilled blood. While Lilith has been invoked by groups who use sex or BDSM tools in their worship of Her, She certainly does not demand this (at least from most). If you are so inclined, there are simple and safe ways to give Her each of these offerings.

Wine can be the simplest to give, provided of course you are of age to purchase it and can afford it (the wine need not be high end stuff). Lilith enjoys wine not mainly as an intoxicating experience but as a blood substitute. The rich red liquid (it must be red wine) can be offered up in a vessel dedicated to Her, using a wine glass, bowl, carafe, or even a dark vase. If so inclined, you may share wine with Her, either in a separate glass or from Her own cup. Try to feel out Her opinion on this—I rarely drink from Her offering vessel but have on certain occasions. As previously noted, Lilith will most likely want this wine to sit on Her altar until it begins to rot and decompose. Remember that She is a goddess of transformation, and like deities associated with death, Lilith makes us aware of the less pleasant parts of the natural cycles of change. After working with Lilith for years, I have become oddly fond of the smell of rotting wine.

As I've witnessed on several occasions, She loves when Her people are naked and covered in wine. When I have seen Her present in the flesh through possessory work, at least one of Her people will be "blessed" via a bottle of red wine emptied over their heads. Of course, there are more subtle ways to anoint yourself in this way. During some solo rituals, I will stand in front of a mirror, take a mouthful of wine, tilt my head back, and allow wine to slowly stream out the sides of my mouth and down my naked body. It's not a lot - just small rivulets of wine. Obviously this is best done on a wood or tile floor that can be wiped clean. An alternative is to get a cheap bottle of red and pour it over yourself in the shower before going to meet Her. Even if you lightly rinse and towel off, the wine scent and essence remains. The wine also tends to make you more aware of your own blood, pulsing continuously through your veins.

Giving blood as an offering can be controversial, but this seems to be because people don't do it safely. In doing research for this book, I was horrified to come across a text that instructed readers to get out their athames and cut themselves for Lilith. *Please do not do this.* Lilith will not be impressed and neither will your E.R. doctors!

The safest way to give blood is by use of diabetic stickers or lancets, commonly used to test one's blood sugar. They can be obtained at most drug stores and pharmacies, although they may be behind the counter (you do not need a prescription). While at the drug store, you should also pick up some individually packaged alcohol wipes. When you wish to give Lilith a blood offering, choose a finger on your non-dominant hand and clean it with the alcohol wipe. Remove the cap from the diabetic sticker and prick the fleshy pad of your finger. Your finger should begin bleeding, sometimes with some gentle rubbing further down the finger, and you do not need more than a few drops of blood. It is the act of offering that matters here, not the amount. Used stickers should be stored in a medical grade sharps container, which can also be obtained at pharmacies. When full, they can be disposed of at your local clinic or hospital.

This blood can be used to anoint candles (before you light them), statues, beads, or other objects on Lilith's altar. On a few occasions, Lilith has prompted me to anoint myself with it (for safety purposes, you should only anoint yourself with your own blood). The drops can also be added to Her wine by holding your finger over the vessel. In this way, the wine becomes even more an offering of yourself to Her.

If you have a menstrual cycle, Lilith will also accept menstrual blood. I have even charged objects for Her in a container of my own collected menstrual blood. You may read in some spiritual sources that menstrual blood should not be used magically as it is "waste blood." There are certainly instances and gods where this is the case. As both a figure of "waste" places and of the shadow side of femininity, however, menstrual blood is absolutely acceptable to Lilith. For those of us that bleed, even touching our own menstrual blood can be seen as dirty, shameful, or embarrassing. Even in some contemporary cultures, men will not touch women at all, just in case they are currently bleeding and are thus "unclean." In reclaiming this mystery that has become a misogynist joke ("what bleeds for seven days but doesn't die?"), we move closer to understanding Lilith's lessons and the cycles of our own body.

If you wish to do any magical or personal work with your own menstrual blood, I would highly recommend using a reusable menstrual cup rather than tampons or maxi pads. Once inserted, these products collect blood and are emptied whenever you would normally change your tampon or maxi pad. The most available model, The DivaCup, can be found online at www.divacup.com. (Despite the overly girly website and pastel colors, it is a high quality and well-researched product!) On a practical level, menstrual cups are great for camping or traveling abroad when you might not be able to carry a week's worth of feminine supplies with you (or be able to dispose of them). Best of all, they are much more eco-friendly. Because they are quite sturdy and reusable for many years, you can literally eliminate decades of used tampons and pads from landfills and septic systems.

Sexual fluids, like blood, are often denigrated as offerings for two main reasons. First, in a world of STDs and HIV, sharing sexual fluids is extremely risky. In working with Lilith, the best way to avoid this is solo sex. Do some reading on using masturbation to raise energy: kundalini or chakra work provides a very good foundation for this. Give Lilith the "fruits" of your labor (again, either dripped into Her wine or on a candle). Working with a partner is generally not recommended unless you practice safe sex or are monogamous partners who have both been tested. Moreover, your partner must also be fully aware of the potential consequences of binding themselves to Lilith. It is simply unethical to use someone as part of an offering without gaining their informed consent.

The second reason people recoil from sexual fluids is that they are seen as the opposite of holy. It's always surprising to me how many people who claim affinity with the sacred exclude sexuality from this arena. Sexual practice is supposed to be cloistered away from all things sacred, lest we dirty up or profane our gods. Denying the sacred aspects of sexuality is to deny the sanctity of the human body. Almost all bodies produce sexual fluids in one way or another. Touching and working with those fluids not only forces us to own what society sees as the messy, "shameful" parts of ourselves; it gives us a powerful and personal tool for spiritual work.

Finally, donations of money, goods, or services to non-profit organizations can be a powerful offering. Lilith may nudge you toward a particular group, but those that provide justice, equality, or protection for women or traditionally marginalized people are recommended, such as Planned Parenthood, the ACLU, GLAD, MADRE, women's shelters, and self-esteem programs for teenage girls. (Note: Lilith has a mixed relationship with young children, so charities that feature them might be best serviced under the auspices of another deity).

Building an Altar

No two altars are identical, even for the same deity. One Lilith's person I know keeps a beautiful red corn snake as a living altar to Her. It must be fed and cared for regularly, just like any other altar. My own Lilith altar—which shifts and transforms over time—sits on my bedroom dresser in front of a large mirror. It includes a naked statue of Her with a large snake wrapped around Her body, based on the painting by John Collier. Although I was a little reluctant to have such a European-looking Lilith representation, I soon realized the statue and I had the same curves. Of course, after a few years, the figure's skin is now completely dark with wine and blood stains.

She has a little bronze owl I found in a market, snake skin, a rattle, and a bed of shiny black stones. Her offering bowl is a former Tibetan singing bowl, which I have filled with sand, wine, or candles. She has an incense holder and enjoys deep, rich scents like patchouli, sandalwood, musk, and Nag Champa (which translated means "Snake Flower"). Next to Her altar is a wooden box which holds jewelry and perfume oils I've dedicated to Her.

I have found that the area around Lilith's altar can be very hard to keep clean. Piles of clothing and papers tend to collect on the floor in front of Her, incense ash coats the surface of the dresser, and the offerings I give Her (usually wine) tend to be left on Her altar until they rot. After a few vain attempts to keep the area tidy, I soon realized that Lilith likes it that way. She will bring messiness, dirt, and pungent odors into your space, just as She brings mess into your life. She is one of the few deities I have encountered who enjoys a dirty altar (as long as this is not the dust of neglect).

Rituals

Perhaps because of how very old She is, Lilith enjoys ritual. This can range from several pages of formal rites to simply standing before Her altar, raising a vessel of wine, and speaking an impromptu prayer from the heart. The purpose of a ritual to Lilith can vary widely and include honoring Her, invoking Her presence or influence, requesting aid, thanking Her, communicating with

Her, dedicating oneself to Her, and marking a point of personal transformation.

You will find that Lilith will make known what form your ritual should take. When I conducted my first ritual to Her, I quickly realized that my old, comfortable practices just wouldn't cut it. If I did what was safe and containable, She couldn't be bothered. If I followed my instincts and ventured into the unknown, She was there. If I expected something to happen a certain way, She trumped it. If I relinquished control and let Her lead, the results were quite powerful. Lilith will not be held at arm's length. She is best approached naked and fleshy—no hiding.

A Short Ritual Template

Below you'll find a simple ritual to invite Lilith in and begin a conversation. Please feel free to adapt this to fit your own purposes and desires. This should be done on an evening when you have at least an hour alone and will not be disturbed.

Create a spiritually conducive atmosphere. Lighting should be dim, preferably just enough to see what you're doing. If you cannot have candles in your space, strings of Christmas lights (white, multicolored, or in an individual color) can provide a good alternative. If you can, light some incense (patchouli, frankincense, musk, sandalwood—anything rich and warm). If you cannot have smoke for whatever reason, consider an essential oil warmer or perfume to diffuse a lighter scent. You may wish to play music, either on a stereo or through headphones if you do not live alone.

What music you associate with Lilith is highly subjective, and I've found Her tastes run from bellydance music to Dead Can Dance and Evanescence to the Dixie Chicks (I know, I was shocked too). Lilith often comes through as an intense force and enjoys a strong, pulsing beat.

When you've prepared your space, it's time to prepare yourself. Take a bath or shower to physically and psychically cleanse yourself. You may wish to use a soap with a particular scent, like sandalwood or patchouli. If you can, cleanse yourself by candlelight (or even a bathroom nightlight). All of your preparations should be made before you cleanse yourself – that way you are stepping into sacred space when you emerge from the bathroom.

If you have one, sit or stand in front of a mirror, naked. Light a candle (red or black is best) and place it in front of you. Ideally there should be no other light except perhaps a few mood candles.

Make an offering of red wine to Her (even in a regular wine glass or the bottle is fine). Hail and welcome Her, either with prepared words or whatever comes from your heart. Speak plainly to Her and tell Her honestly why you're there. Allow yourself to sit in silence for at least a few moments after this, open and receptive to Her. You should have a journal and pen at your side in case She begins to communicate with you. It can be very difficult to remember things after the fact.

Pay attention to your own face in the mirror and how your body feels. For most people, She tends to speak *through you*. You will feel Her within yourself before sensing Her around you. She may prompt you to dance to the music (naked) in front of the mirror. Let yourself go and try to lose all inhibitions; it's a good way to invite Her to move through your body.

In lieu of or in addition to dancing, you may chant for Her. Repeat Her name (or any title or relationship you associate with Her: Mother, Sister, Goddess, Queen, etc.)with focused intent, gazing into the mirror. You may also slip into a meditative state, although I've found this to be less effective with Her than with other deities. Lilith tends to come into our space more easily than pulling us into Hers. You may feel the urge to do divination during the ritual. Using tools like tarot cards can help open the lines of communication with Her if Her presence is not clear.

Be open to spontaneous action and spontaneous emotion. Beware of promising things to Her you cannot deliver—She takes such oaths seriously. You will have a sense when the ritual seems to be winding down. Ask if She has any parting words for you. Thank Her for Her presence, even if it was not what you expected.

After the ritual, you will need to ground yourself, whether you feel energized or exhausted. Eat a piece of whole grain bread and peanut butter, some meat, a hard boiled egg, or something with protein and complex carbs. Drink lots of water and get a full night's rest.

Part III: Songs of Lilith

for Wisdom

The pen and the book, the blood and the wine.
These things are not contrary.

I am an owl perched on skulls.
My sharp voice pierces the night.
Yellow eyes fix themselves on you
Arresting
Questioning
Probing.

You cannot know me,
not unless you have turned your own eyes inward,
searching the darkness there.

You will spill a fathomless measure of black, inky blood
in search of me,
only to find yourself, suspended in a womb,
dreaming of your own awakening.

for Night

I am movement, pulsing, the hunt at night.
The seduction.
Meet me in the dark places.

for Barrenness

I have razed your little village to the ground.
The earth lies scorched and smoking beneath your feet.
Around you lies the ashes of all you clung to.

Only now can you see the path leading you from this place,
For it is the only thread of earth remaining
I have not destroyed.

As you find your way, you will give thanks for the lesson.
Your village was always barren.
I have revealed its emptiness to you.
Now you possess only the spark I planted within you,
A keen hunger, gnawing from within.

for Magic

I am exceptionally old.
Primitive.
One of the first.
The First.
I must be greeted and praised and given offerings in the Old Way.
These ways are lost.

But you may smell them.
The smell of rotting wine,
The pungent tang of blood in the air.
These are the signs of my holy presence.

for Wings

Feel the brush of my wings against your cheek.
Wear them as you stalk the streets, spreading behind and above you.
Feel the itch between your shoulder blades as they quiver beneath
tightly drawn skin.

Remember: there is always a back door—in and out.
Even in Eden.

for Mysteries

I am the snake moving through you when you dance

I am the wine flowing through you when you drink

I am the wind pushing and caressing you when you walk

I am the dark Maria and the light

The black and white Madonna

I am thought and emotion holding hands

I am everything

I am the world and its crying

I am the first woman and the last

Serpent and dove

Outcast and holy mother

for Life Blood

I am the ache of blood.
I am the sting and the pull and the throb of life.
Truly, my appetite is voracious.

I cry tears of blood.
Champion of the bleeding and the wounded
Reserve of strength
I am the last ounce of power
of rage
of survival
that keeps you alive.

I too have longed for death—and lived.
I refuse to die.

Part IV: Devotions
Invocations and Invitations

Prayer to the Mother of All Time
Lillith ThreeFeathers Lewis

Mother of all time,

You who existed in the mists of the past,

I ask you to be here

Bring your love and wisdom into my life.

I long to be in your presence.

Queen of Shadows,

You see into the dark places.

Help me to find the way to my true self,

to my rightful path.

Queen of Light,

You know all my joys and pains,

Bring me strength.

You who see beyond the shadows.

Bring me awareness.

Invocation to Mother Lilith

Lillith ThreeFeathers Lewis

My lady Lilith,
All knowing dark mother.
Thou who stood at the roots of the Tree of Life —
and stands there still,
I call to you.
Thou who gave us the spark of passion,
I call to you.
Keeper of the mysteries,
Thy feet stand on the lion,
Thy wings encompass the owl's wisdom,
and the hawk's meaning.
In the past,
You were highest priestess of the Temple.
To you every knee bent.
Every tongue gave homage to you.
Thou who healed the returning warriors
of the ravages of war
and softened their hearts
so they could return to their loved ones.
Words cannot express Thy grace,
Thy beauty,
the power of Thy touch.
My Lady, we remember and recognize Thee.
Holy winged one
Clothed in light,
Lady of the night,

Help us tonight.

Darkness beneath the shadows,

Light of first breath,

Queen of the Universe,

Great Mother,

We pray Thee,

Join us in this place

And bless us with thy loving presence.

Encounters

S. Reicher

When first You came to me,
it was as the serpent
slithering through the garden
of my own half-acknowledged desires.
Lilith.
Even Your name was lush with the promise
of danger.
But what did I know?
I still thought chanting and praying were enough.

When first You came, I watched from afar,
and I saw black secrets dancing in Your eyes.
I smelled the musk
of desolation and sinew
the enticement
of a stone-cold furious will.
I saw the shadows You made
in the mirror of my mind:
A woman with the jeweled eyes of some great snake,
slithering through the darkness,
spiraling around the thousand-hued emerald boughs
of the Tree – beckoning
atop the seat of wisdom,
from which You had never once been unthroned.
The Queen of Heaven Herself bowed before You.

The second time, I watched You
Ancient vampire,
sucking sense and sex
out of Your unwitting prey
Baruch Atah....sweet Seductress.
I watched as You took Your worshipper
to his knees in supplication.
Great Devourer, he too chose to eat
Of Your fruit
and be devoured.

The third time, Searing One,
You came as Sirocco Dancer,
with the hot desert wind as Your breath,
and the cleansing devastation of its heat
to mark Your passing
merciless as flensing knives
dancing across unsuspecting skin.
That ancient garden almost seemed safe
in contrast.
Almost.

And then You came for me,
winged, hungry, fierce
like a great owl,
hidden in darkness,
ferreting out prey
only it can see.
You did not take the channel

prepared by Other Gods.

You made Your own,

in the dark, twisting pathways of my heart.

You opened me as though with the crimson kiss

of a razor tailed whip

and I sang Your song for another.

I see You now, Seductress of Angels,

Adoration of the flesh.

I hear the soft, silky whisper

of wings as You pass.

What You have to teach,

would turn ancient grimoires to ash,

and render mad the davening of mystics.

Baruch Atah

Lilith.

In the Tree: Lilith the Owl

Tree Climbing

Natalie Long

She-snake who lived in the Huluppu
Spoke the four-letter name and flew
From Malkuth-Eden into Yesod
To mate with Lucifer, in the land of Nod.
And there together they hatched a plan
to bring the fire of Kether into Man.
To Eden they built a middle path
The way of the Priestess, across Da'ath.
Lilith dwells still in the tree
And she has shown the way to me.

Lilith[30]
Kenny Klein

By the shores of the Tigris
Where the Hebrews were enslaved
There reigned a shinning Goddess
Lilith is her name

She flew through the deserts
As an owl so bright and gay
She slithered as a serpent
Lilith is her name

They call her the diamond
They speak of her bright flame
They call her Queen of Heaven
Lilith is her name

They say she dwelled in Eden
When Adam was newly made
As a snake she roamed the garden
Lilith is her name

She wears a cloak of feathers
She wears a crown of flame
She'll catch you in her labyrinth

---

30 From the album, "Meet Me In The Shade of the Maple Tree," by Kenny Klein

Lilith is her name

They call her the diamond
They speak of her bright flame
They call her Queen of Heaven
Lilith is her name

So come ye bold young sailors
You soldiers and travelers the same
And swear you to a Goddess
Lilith is her name

She'll make the bard to strike the string
She'll bring the poet fame
She will carry you to heaven
Lilith is her name

They call her the diamond
They speak of her bright flame
They call her Queen of Heaven
Lilith is her name

The Tale of the Screech Owl Girl

Tahni J. Nikitins

What does the screech owl weave
In the night time star's dream
Hanging over the world dome
Where the jackals sing
And hyenas laugh?
Where the night-time beasts roam
And the satyrs drink and dance
Is where she, too, will lounge
When her weaving picture's done.

Open up your jewelry box, my daughter—
The one with the pearl inlay, and porcelain ballerina
Who spins upon a single toe;
The one which sings so softly
And once did lull you to sleep on crying nights;
The one which holds that part of you
That would wear short skirts
And tight red shirts
The part that would dance with men at night
Drink her fill and eat her favorite foods.
Open up your jewelry box, my daughter
And look carefully upon her.

The screech owl does lay her mournful scream

Upon us as we sleep

To shake us from our dreams

To bring us to where the moon reigns high

Where the wolves bay at one another

From either side of the quickly flowing river.

We are the crayfish in this scene

To drown or not to drown

We must swim up this stream.

Within your jewelry box there is a mirror

Which fits as a key in a lock to your palm;

Which has a back of white gold

Formed carefully as poppy petals

Cradling its treasured reflection.

Oh dear daughter of mine

Gaze into this looking glass

And look into your eyes

Look into them deeply

Until at last you'll see her there.

They would bound the screech owl's wings

Pull the feather from her flesh

And fold her into porcelain.

They'd melt her down and pour her as a ballerina

And lock her in pearl-inlaid box

Complete with lullabies.

Beside your mirror there lies a comb

Carved so carefully out of the finest bone.

My daughter, my dear

Lift this to your flaming hair

And loose the gnarled knots, the dirt and leaves

That had collected there;

Lift this to your flaming hair and comb the locks

Watching yourself in the mirror,

Collect all the strength and beauty to be possessed

To shine like moons inside your eyes.

The screech owl has

So many sad songs to sing

Her words did catch my ears

Like a hook in the gills of a fish

And dragged me from my cradle

Whereabouts I picked up her solemn tale.

At last within your jewelry box, my love

You'll find a seed to be sown.

Do plant it in the soot black earth

And wait for it to grow.

The life that springs from tree sprigs spring

With much a price to pay.

Pluck the fruits from the branches

Of your well tended crops

Comb these knots and roots and things from your hair

Hesitate not to admire your own skin
And eat the sweetest reddest fruits you'd find.

Let me tell you now, my injured child
The tale so woeful and grim
Of the rape of the screech owl girl
And the child she buried within.

Sweet soft child of mine
Look yourself in the mirror
Comb the last of leaves from your hair
Wipe it from your mind.
Pretend the bruises are not there
And look upon your skin
As pale as any marble's ever been.
Admire the softness of your breasts
The elegance of your sweetened neck
The moon-like shimmer in your eyes
The rubies which repose upon your lips
And wonder at your soft-sweet thighs
Liquid as fresh milk
And find your feet amazing, sweet and small
And toughened to the earthen stones
And gaze upon your tapered fingers
Upon your strengthened palm
Which may create anything
At any will you'd have.

Now daughter you listen to me
And you listen to me well.
This is the reason you'll never see day
This is the reason you'll never know night:
These dreams which we so boldly weave
So quickly turn upon their stitch-master maker
To swallow them up in nightmare.

They called the screech owl girl demon
For from her loins were born these words:
All yes's and all no's
And when they came upon her
She dared to push them back
For rather that she would
Hold her place beside them rather than beneath them.

And so each babe she bore
They tore off of her breast.
They threw them in the fires, you see,
and drown them in the seas.
Wailing wild the screech owl girl became
And in her terribly fury
She tore their babies from their breasts
Just as they'd dare to tear hers
And at last she had become
The demon they had feared.

Within her daughters, all of us

Lies a seed of hers

To teach us of our strengths

But taught to bury it deep

We often never live to see it grow.

This for you I'd have not, my child.

But rather I'd have you see this seed sown

And live to see it grow

To witness the leaves unfurl to the sun

And the roots to climb within the earth

And spread throughout the ground;

I'd have for you a world where

Sex was magic, and magic not taboo;

But this world is not so.

The screech owl saw this sight

Where pulled out of her bed

They cut her golden hair

Called her "whore of whores"

And laid her out for all to see

And when she pushed them back from her

When she scratched and bit and fought

They called her wild and crazy witch

Damned and hated by their god.

And so I've seen you in the woods

Laying soft and broken

Weeping where my hand cannot reach

To dry your bruising eyes.
Beside you I do see
The pearl inlaid wooden box
Its contents on the ground.
Gather them up my dear child
And take them under your arm.
Together we shall throw them in the fire
And I'll hold you while they burn.

Your mirror has been shattered
Your comb it has been broken
Your seed was stolen from you
And so you'll dance nor sing no more.

Goodnight, goodnight, forever goodnight.
Lift your arms and shake your fiery mane
And let me sing to you
The tale of the screech owl girl
For here I part with you
Before you've come to be.

Goodbye, goodbye, forever goodbye
Sweet child of mine
And if you see the screech owl girl
Be she man, woman or child
Maiden, weeping mother or crone

Sit beside her and give her a listen—

Can you imagine the tales she'll tell?

In the Garden: Lilith the Snake

Hands Outstretched
Anya Kless

If only there had been no Adam.

If only it had remained a woman and her God
in Paradise.

Did she seduce Him, as they say,
to learn the secret name?

Or did He give it freely,
in a moment of terrible compassion?

"This is your out."

Submission or exile
Man's subject or God's rival

She laughed as the tears fell,
stunned by His ingenuity
His generosity
His cruelty

It was an easy choice.
What woman could lie beneath a man

after knowing a god?

She spoke the name.
Her wings sprouted like black cancer.
She did not look back as she cleared the walls.
She found the desert and her demons.
Her pain festered, her rage eternal.

Did she discover her serpent form
And slither back into Eden for revenge?

Or did He give it to her,
to become the sacred adversary,
to take up the terrible mantle of all taboo?

Hail the desert queen
Hail She who will not be tamed
Hail the annihilating feminine

Hail Lilith, mother of demons
Hail She, beloved of Yahweh

you on me

Mai'a Williams

you and me eve

we can be the first no
the you-boys-can-go-fuck-yourself
the middle finger to thin-lipped figures
on the sidewalk as we twist our hips
and make them cry

we can demand to be satisfied
refuse to be the dutiful daughters
on our knees

don't smile when we ain't happy
nod when we don't agree
no more
that ain't got to be we

we can be a blues song
on a moonless night
when everything ain't close to right
and drink hard liquor in hard bars
like old vets wailing out stories
of hell fire, brimstone,
and childhood's blood-soaked dreams

laughing full belly

we can be greater than gods

let the blinders fall
and carry each other's shadows
our backs to the sun

let me pluck you like a golden apple
peel away your skin
and eat until i make you scream

we can be
the last word

free.

In which we discuss descent

Sara Amis

Once there was a tree, in a garden. Once there was a woman.

Once there was a serpent, who was wise.

He said, Know this. The sweet taste of apples. The bite of a sharp
tooth.

If you want to be alive, if you want to know your own mind,

If you want a will of your own,

If you want, if you want, if you taste desire—

You will feel joy. You will feel pain.

You will know love. You will know regret.

That's how it is.

You can share my power, O Woman,

of drawing spirit into form,

of making the world anew, giving birth

to a will independent of your own

entrained in matter like yours, and mine.

If you do this thing, you will also create death.

That light you give, *dar a luz,*

Will one day be extinguished. You must choose

not only for yourself, but for all of them.

And some, who do not love their freedom

will despise you for it.

The woman shrugged. She was only three days old,

but she knew a setup when she saw one;

A chessboard with only one move.

She could stand in that unchanging garden forever,

pretty figure in a tapestry, or she could get going.

Elder Sister, all dust and whirlwinds,

had already blown this joint, red hair waving like a pirate flag:

No quarter.

The least she could do in her turn was take a bite.

Leaving the Garden, Becoming the Snake

Anya Kless

She came quickly and stronger than she'd ever let me feel Her before. The energy in the space throbbed with Her, and I later learned that my poor housemate, who is quite sensitive to spiritual energy, had been unable to sleep until the ritual was over. She began speaking right away.

"I will make you a Hell to men."

She took me back to the first ritual I had done for Her on the ground, charging a candle with my body.

She is the Queen of cunts and pain and blood.

This tattoo marks my dedication to Her. She will always have a piece of me. I am formally entering into Her service now. She has awakened my thirst for understanding through pain, fear, and power. She has the throaty laugh of a sated predator.

Lilith, I sacrifice to you my old notions of the sacred feminine. You are my sacred feminine now.

I dance for Her, writhing like a snake, and hold my body in the stillness of Her sacred poses. Her palms are always open. It is in one of these poses, palms up in supplication, that She opens me to understanding Her own pain.

I know what it was to leave the Garden. I finally understand the pain and desolation of the desert. It was not what She expected.

"I sacrificed Paradise for freedom. Now you are leaving the Garden as well."

As I cried silently for Her, my body shook and tears fell. My back shook. I gave Her my tears and my understanding.

To be alone, but refusing to be on Her knees. Never on Her knees.

In every previous ritual I had done with Her, I always had a clear sense of when She had left. Not this time. She never fully left. She's still inside me. In the right light, you can see Her in my eyes.

I rebuilt her altar in my bedroom, in front of the mirror. I filled Her offering bowl with red wine and offered up a prayer of praise to Her. I charged and lit a candle for Her. I marked my body with her wine until it looked like a canvas of cuts and welts.

"In the old days, when a woman was given to Lilith, she would be flogged or whipped until she bled. Her palms would be made open to show her willing acceptance. Then she would become the snake and dance.

"You have already been flogged and beaten for me. Now, pain is your payment to be my priestess. Will you pay the price?"

I am Her priestess. I have paid.

Queen of Outcasts: Lilith the Gender Outlaw

Chosen

Aiden Fyre

For some, accepting the call to serve and honor comes without question or doubt. For others, like myself, skepticism and uncertainty cloud our willingness to accept that the gods have chosen us to do their bidding and be an instrument of Their will.

Riding the human form so that She could walk among us on Earth, Lilith, the dark goddess of the middle world, confirmed what I had started to suspect but feared was mere fantasy and delusion. As I watched the ritual from a distance, Her eyes met mine before leaving the tent and striding up to me. I felt Her eyes bore into me like a predator sizing up its prey; seducing me with Her eyes, She drew me in until I could no longer hear the others around me. Captivated by Her, the night closed in around me and filled me with lust. Drunken with desire, She placed Her arm around me and pulled me towards Her bosom. Offering me wine and then anointing my head, She smirked seductively as the fluid, red as blood, trickled down my face. Under the stars at Cauldron Farm, I knew that Lilith had claimed me as Hers.

As the goddess of lust and vitality, Lilith empowers us to seek and share pleasure. We honor Her when we bask in the pleasures of the flesh and give in to our desires. It is Her energy that courses through me when I allow passion to fuel me. Bridging the worlds of earth and sky, mind and body, Lilith has also helped me to delve deep into my convictions about sexuality.

A shape-shifter and hermaphrodite, Lilith gives birth to transformation and change as a transmasculine deity. She, along with the transfeminine god, Shiva Ardhanarishvara, give me strength and permission to delve into the many facets within me and morph at will. As I flux between genders and inhabit the middle space between worlds, I feel Their influence and power. Without a doubt, it is this transcendence of gender and conventional sexuality that has defined who I am and directly impacted my relations with people and the work that I do.

Kinky. Queer. GenderQueer. Each transgression from the norm has led me to where I am today. Being on the fringe has helped me to become self-aware and strong. A source of power and pain, being All and None has gifted me with an enormous capacity for empathy, compassion, and the ability to morph and walk between the worlds.

Called for a purpose I have yet to fully comprehend, I am following the path of sacred gender, sex, and ordeal. It is Her work that I do. It is Her voice that is heard when I speak of erotic freedom. Each time I part my lips to kiss or my legs to fuck, I am sharing her message of passion and pleasure. When I compel others to live in their purpose and dare them to question the unspoken rules, I am spreading Her message. As I inspire others to indulge in the joy of the body, to stretch the confines of gender and sexuality, and to delve into their own beliefs and sexual mores, I honor Her.

Sometimes we do not get to choose our path because it is chosen for us. Called to a purpose we may not fully understand, the call to serve may come like a beacon from afar that we can barely discern but know is there. Yet, other times, it can be clear and without question. Indeed, the journey to honor and serve can be just as ambivalent as the gods themselves.

Scirocco Goddess

Raven Kaldera

Lilith first came to me when I was living as a bearded, hairy woman. She came like a *scirocco,* and that's how I always pictured her – a dervish-whirl of sandy colors, her scimitar flicking through the air in circles too quick to see, the death of a thousand cuts. Others have met the seductive femme-fatale Lilith, which is perhaps her more "biblical" face, but for me she was a creature of the barren desert sands. Her body was female, but hairy like mine. She wore ass-legs, or sometimes goat-legs. I never saw beneath her skirts, and I never dared to ask.

She came to me as an interrogator. It was only later that I discovered that she had vague associations with the Greek Sphinx, the monster who asked hard questions and ate you if you couldn't answer them. The questions were about my gender, my future, my assumptions, and most especially my sexuality. *What do you want that you don't dare to think about? What do you want that you'd never tell your lovers? Why can't you be in your body when you have sex? If you could be in your body, how would things be different? What do you intend to do about your situation? Because, you know, it can't go on like this.*

I was avoidant, and I tried to blow her off. I had spent much of my life up to that point in serious denial of my issues – unhappily so, but at least it was a comfortable, fatalistic sort of unhappiness, the sort where you don't have to add any new struggles to the existing ones because it wouldn't work anyway, right? I'd been approached by other goddesses before, and I'd gotten a feeling of "sent over to talk some sense into you" from each one – Artemis, Cerridwen, etc. – but I blew them off, too, because I could. The goddess who actually owned me, well, I didn't know her name then, and she remained a shadowy figure in the background … waiting.

But Lilith was the first one who would not be put off. When I ignored her, she shook up my entire world by ripping a hole in my head and possessing me. I mean that quite literally; she rode my body like a horse and danced it into exhaustion. *Now will you shut up and listen to me?* I had no choice. I listened. I struggled. I spent six months in an Umbanda house, learning to be a horse, to carry deities properly … and like it or not, I dealt with my growing gender issues.

When I read about Lilith, I found her source material to be filled with contradictions. Part of that was because she seemed to cross mythologies and cosmologies, turning up in a variety of Semitic-origin tales. Some things stood out, though, chillingly. I read that she was called the Hairy Goddess, covered in hair like an animal – a trait which stood out against all the more modern sensibilities of her being shown as a feminine, if aggressive, "pretty" demon. (But, of course, she's one of the shapeshifting Gods, so she can look like whatever she wants, I'm sure.) I read the warnings about her overwhelming libido, and the hermaphroditic gender-switching children that she was supposed to have birthed by the hundreds – the incubi/succubi. I read about her gift of barrenness – coming between a couple at night in their own bed and making them both unable to breed. I recognized these traits, with a sinking feeling in the pit of my stomach. I knew that she had not been sent for no reason.

When I hit puberty, my (heretofore female) body went crazy with a plethora of secondary sex characteristics. I grew breasts and grew hair on them, I got irregular and painful menses and clitoral growth, my hips broadened and my voice cracked and hair grew on my chin. I was shapeshifting into something weird and terrible and awe-inspiring. I would discover later that the name of my intersex condition was secondary congenital adrenal hyperplasia, but at the time all I knew was that my mother freaked out, took me to a series of doctors, got me put on estrogens, and told me that I had a "hormone problem". It was hammered into my head: I must do everything in my power to stay female. My mother, who believed in female superiority and had said that she could never love a son, wanted to make sure that I was pointed in the right direction, permanently. (I was lucky that she was too much of a prude to ever ask to see my teenage genitalia, and I was too fearful to mention what was happening to them.)

So in my twenties, I read the stories of Lilith, and something clicked in me on a deep level. I knew what it was to live in a female body that was hairy, infertile, and lustful (due to high testosterone levels that drove my libido up). The myth of Lilith was reflected in my medical condition … or, possibly, my medical condition was reflected in the myth of Lilith. I wonder, still, when I think about those uncomfortable interstices between human history and experience and divine Otherworldliness, how much of the wondrous experience of being a monster like me went into the stories of this ambivalent goddess who was likewise treated like a monster for so many centuries.

The most shameful thing of all was that I was living with a husband and seeing a boyfriend, neither of whom knew about my medical condition. I took my hormones, I plucked hair, I kept silent. *No one must know.* It was my terrible secret. It wasn't just fear of rejection; it was a deep knowing that if I faced it and its spiritual implications enough to tell them, it would set off a chain of earthquakes in my life that would shatter it entirely.

Lilith never told me anything, or ordered me to do anything. She only asked me questions, more and more questions. *Do you really believe that this is what you're supposed to be doing for the rest of your life? Striving for a goal that's physically impossible for you, and that you hate anyway? Who are you still trying to impress? Your mother? Is she worth throwing your life away for? Your friends? If they're real friends, won't they care about you no matter what your body looks like? The women's community? If they'd reject you for this, well, what does that say about them and their level of spiritual evolution? So they have no idea how to deal with intersexuals, should that affect your decision? Or is it that you're afraid of being seen as unattractive, as an ugly hairy creature that no one will fuck? That's it, isn't it? Just vanity? Is vanity really worth your peace of mind? And really … would it be so terrible to be alone?*

The questions shook things loose in me, even when I didn't answer them. It was like being flayed alive by a sandstorm. It took my armor and my clothing off, and then my skin. I stood naked and desolate in front of my own shame. It was the first step in a long process that led to me going off of the estrogens that were ruining my health and seeing what my body would do on its own. (The husband and the boyfriend both vanished, as I'd feared they would, but other lovers who accepted me as I was appeared in my life right on schedule.) Further down that path was a full masculinization and a legal sex reassignment, an entire relinquishing of my right to the country of women, a country I'd secretly crept into with no right to it. The changes in my body also meant relinquishing Lilith's willingness to be carried by me – she was fine with a vehicle that was female of center, but when I moved permanently across that line (although still just as close to the middle) she bluntly told me that she was done with me.

It's strange to me that she would have encouraged me to do something that would make me useless to her, but it's one of her qualities: Being true to yourself is more important than anything else, including the needs of Gods. There are other Gods I've known before and since who would not agree with that proposition; who would stretch the limits of someone's comfort if that person's discomfort would be useful toward their long-term goals, who would put those goals above any single human's personal needs, and expect them to be honored that their suffering helped so many others. Lilith, on the other hand, didn't seem to be about long-term goals. She was about honesty in the Now, in the Here, in the Moment. *Are you seeing yourself Now?* she would ask.

Her touch tears down authority, like so many other Gods of Chaos. Her voice drives you to question everything. While I was destined to live under Authority, Lilith at least helped to make sure that it was not any kind of human Authority – and, it is true, all my residual dependence on human opinions had to be cleared away to make room for the eventual divine Authority, which would not be hers. I don't know if she even approved of my final Wyrd, but that wouldn't matter – her own relentless drive for internal questioning was irrelevant to my future. She didn't care what I would become, except that if she would help it, that future me would be someone dedicated to self-honesty, whatever my Wyrd might be.

Are you seeing yourself Now? It's something that we could all take a little more seriously.

What I Learned in Bootcamp

Anya Kless

For many, Lilith is the unofficial goddess of BDSM, a patron saint of whips and black latex. Some (consciously or not) transform their scenes into rites, making offerings of perversity, pain, and pleasure. My initiation into the world of BDSM served Her in two ways. It brought me in contact with various partners who became teachers or teaching opportunities. Through my interactions with them, I gained a cross-section of physical, mental, and psychological skill sets. Additionally, it took me on a revealing tour through my own fears, insecurities, and dark places. The internal became external—scenarios I had desired or feared (or hadn't even realized I desired or feared) were suddenly placed before me. In retrospect, I can see those years as the first serious leg of my journey down the ordeal path, a method of growth in which the journeyer learns and progresses through a series of challenging experiences. As a spiritual path, ordeal work is also a means of coming closer to one's gods. In this light, my first few years exploring BDSM served as a specialized priestess bootcamp (excuse the pun). I didn't just learn how to wield a cane—I learned what that cane could mean, where it could take you, what spiritual use it might have. While I understand the huge difference between work and play, I am proud of where I learned many of my skills.

It's no coincidence that I become a priestess of Lilith during the same period I learned to Top. I learned from the bottom up, spending a few years as a submissive and then a slave before realizing this was not all of who I was. After a few years, I was luckily enough to find a compatible partner willing to explore his own submissive tendencies. Although we switched on occasion, it was those F/m exchanges (Female dominant, male submissive) that pushed us both deeper than we expected. Over the course of those two years, I often felt Lilith's guiding hand. My relationship with this partner has since ended, but I occasionally look back at the journal I kept during that time. The excerpts below, all from the first year of that relationship, trace an arch in my development as Her priestess and in my understanding of my own needs and desires.

Entry #1: The rush

He has the body of a top—tall, muscled, strong—but seeing that body kneeling before you, bound and eager, is all the more arousing. Seeing his earnest face as he struggles to take my boots off with his teeth. Watching his whole body shake in nervous anticipation. I could get used to this. As he bends over a chair, still bound, I stroke his back and whisper in his ear.

"You're shaking."

"Yes Miss."

"Why is that?"

"I'm nervous, Miss."

"Why?"

"Because I want to please you, Miss."

"No need to be nervous about that. You please me just as you are."

"Thank you, Miss."

A moment passes in silence.

"You're still shaking, darling."

"Yes Miss."

"Why now?"

"I'm nervous what you'll do next, Miss."

I laugh. "That's a much better reason."

In some ways, it's so much easier being on the bottom, especially if you're a beginner. You have to be open and honest, but you're not calling the shots, gauging your partner's physical and emotional state, deciding what happens next. As I soon learned, however, being on Top is also incredibly rewarding, especially if your partner is new to all this. Being able to take them places they've never been. Doing things to them they never thought would actually happen.

Even at the beginning of what was meant to be a "switch" relationship, I often found myself Topping for weeks at a time, an arrangement that seemed to come out of his need. After we'd built a foundation of trust in the relationship, he made himself vulnerable enough to tell me that he *needed* to be on the bottom: to serve me, to be tortured by me, to please me. Ironically, it was probably the submissive part of me that initially agreed to this. I wanted to give him what he wanted. Soon, however, I was astounded at how much I loved it, how little I missed being on the other side of things. Besides the pleasurable rush of the scene, I was getting a crash course in Topping. It wasn't until months later that I admitted to him He was my first submissive.

Entry #2: More than just the boots

I take charge, subtly. I'm learning its all in the voice—who's asking the questions, what tone they're using. My Top voice is actually rather soft and silky. I don't yell. Velvet covered steel, if you want to get metaphorical. She is definitely in there, snaking around. When I'm on Top, I'm stern and cruel, but I am also generous. I'm clear that I have chosen him because of how much he pleases me. He is eager, slightly shy, and devoted. It's kind of an Evil Queen / devoted slave dynamic. Or Samson and Delilah. He has all the strength, but I control it.

After a good warm up, I find bungee cords on the floor. With one cord, I bind his legs together and make him lie face down on the bed. With the other, I make a large loop and take a swing at his bare ass. Starting slowly, I bring him up to the sweet spot, near tears. I relish the energy—as does She—as his body begins to sing and explode.

Later, he acts in my service. Seeing him kneeling at the end of a leash, hands behind his head, is a stunning sight. He has already perfected proper kneeling posture: knees apart, back straight, head up, eyes down. I walk around him, boots clicking on the hardwood floor. I tug on the leash from time to time, surveying my prize. He looks like a roman slave as I begin the interrogation.

"Do you know why you keep your eyes down?"

"No Miss."

"Because it's a privilege to look at me."

A loud pop sounds as the end of the leash hits his chest. A gasp.

"Do you understand?"

"Yes Miss."

"Good."

During our scenes, I often felt Lilith. Sometimes Her energy lingered around the edges like that of a spectator. At other times She felt immediate, as if She were using my form as a shell. Since Her arrival, I have interacted with Lilith by opening myself to Her presence. I don't know if I would call this "aspecting" or "shadowing," but it does change my appearance and my energy. After working with Lilith for a few years, I could call Her into me and hold Her for periods of time. While Topping, I had to be quite careful to hold Her back—even as he drank Her in as much as I did. The biggest clue to Lilith's presence is the change to my eyes. He used to comment on their intensity after a scene. There were moments he had a hard time looking me in the eye.

Entry #3: States of abjection

"On a scale of 1 to 10, may I have a 9, please, Miss? I need it."

"I'll keep that in mind."

"Actually, pain 8, humiliation 9.5, Miss."

"I see."

As my skills and confidence grew under Lilith's tutelage, my boy proceeded further and further down the path of submission. Humiliation became a fixation of his, and I finally learned one possible reason why. One night, he admitted that he had been badly bullied as a teenager. Initially, I was puzzled. Why would someone who had been humiliated by his peers seek out that same experience voluntarily? And eroticize it? Through our scenes, I came to understand that he needed to face those ingrained feelings of humiliation. He needed to confront what had happened to him and see that he could survive it. He needed someone to see him in that position and not reject him. He needed to reimagine what place humiliation held in his life.[31] Yet even people who don't have a history of bullying and abuse can be drawn to degrading experiences, which can seem puzzling or even sick from the outside. Why?

Another reason, which I see as directly tied to Lilith, is the appeal of the abject, literally "the state of being cast off." Abjection is the twin state of horror and fascination we feel when we realize the truth of our bodies. In *Volatile Bodies,* Elizabeth Grosz observes, "Abjection is a sickness at one's own body, at the body beyond that 'clean and proper' thing." The abject body also repeatedly violates its own borders—leaking snot, sexual fluids, excrement, sweat, blood—and disrupts our wish for physical self-control. In *Horror And The Monstrous Feminine,* Barbara Creed gives a definition which, to me, reeks of Lilith: "The place of the abject is where meaning collapses, the place where I am not. The abject threatens life, it must be radically excluded from the place of the living subject, propelled away from the body and deposited on the other side of an imaginary border which separates the self from

---

31 It should be noted that he was also seeing a therapist at the time to process these issues. While our scenes helped him, they did not take the place of professional assessment.

that which threatens the self." Who better to teach us that our bodies are much messier than we like to admit? Or that the boundaries of selfhood that protect us from others and the outside world are far more permeable? Who else but a "cast off" goddess of waste places and shadows?

Entry #4: The myth of the dominant woman

I've been thinking a lot about my two past Doms, my kink teachers. I am playing back what I learned from them, how they taught me, what they believed. I am trying to sift the wheat from the chaff. Unfortunately I don't have an all-knowing Domme teacher (unless you count Lilith). I am thinking over one past statement in particular: "Dommes are ultimately just as submissive. Everything they do is catered to the male's needs." This statement assumes that the Domme gets no satisfaction from what they do. Yes, there are Pro Dommes, but I don't do this for cash. I know what he wants from me. What is it that I want from him? How do I take my pleasure? Where do I base my power? How do I draw out this authentic part of myself instead of just embodying a stereotype?

These questions haunted me for quite a while, and for the duration of our relationship, I don't think they ever fully went away. Intellectually, I knew what I was supposed to learn from this stint of being on top: that this relationship was not just his personal session: therapeutic, pleasurable, or otherwise. Those things were great, but this was a two way street and for fuck's sake, I was in charge! I knew I needed to make demands of him. I needed to make him earn what he wanted. But for what purpose?

One of the biggest realizations Lilith brought to me through this relationship was how little I knew about what I wanted. Perhaps that's why submission had been relatively easy for me: I didn't have to think about my own needs and desires. I could just focus on someone else's. When it came time for me to voice these things myself, I didn't even know where to start. As a lifelong people pleaser, I had never even really thought about what I wanted. It just wasn't part of the equation. Now, I needed to dig through the back room of my psyche and find those unvoiced desires I locked away. Otherwise, our dynamic would fall apart, and I would become merely a service Top, there to fulfill his needs.

I also needed to consider why I had hidden them in the first place. What was the worst that would happen if I voiced my desires? They'd be ridiculed. I'd realize my partner couldn't fulfill them. Perhaps, if I made a demand on my partner that didn't turn him on, he'd lose interest. Maybe he'd leave. Ultimately, this was exactly how the relationship ended. I asked for something he wouldn't give me, something I needed. As terrifying as it was to ask, it also gave me an immense sense of relief. I knew that I had done all I could. I had voiced my need. I learned that if this ended the relationship, perhaps our time together was no longer fruitful. Looking back at Lilith's stories, I now realize this as one of Her most difficult yet essential lessons: knowing when to leave.

Queen of Blood: Lilith the Demon, Lilith the Vampire

Lilith

Christina Lythia H.

Lilith, Queen of Demons,
Encircled by temptation.
Mistress of the darkened moon,
The werewolves' only savior.

Serpentine in manner,
But not in feature,
Persuasive, penetrating voice.
Whispering her secrets.

Her sweet decadence,
A sanguine flavor,
Spills from her snow white throat,
I desire to be hers, forever.

A dark deadly angel,
Whirling through the night,
She is the queen of free women,
An undying Dark Goddess.

The Eternal Shadows

Christina Lythia H.

Soulless eyes of the demon gaze into mine,
Seeing inner power that resides within their bicolored depths.
The demon looks at me.
It whispers many secrets.

It whispers of
Screams that echo through old dark rooms,
Shadows engulfing the essence of trapped souls.

It shows me a
Midnight butterfly,
Lying dead on the floor.
Blood oozing through its wings
That will never again soar.

It points to
Vermillion stains on the ground from pierced hearts,
Scarlet rains through out the dark shadows.
Faeries dancing in twisted spirals.
A dragon's fire burning alone.

It gives me a
Demon wolf's pelt lying in the blood.
A crimson raven that flies only for me.
A rabbit's head, torn by the soulless eyed demon,
It rests in the inky blackness,

It's an offering for me to take.

It makes me listen to
A place on the edge of sanity where a silent scream erupts,
Blood staining the screamers fingers an angry red,
Red like a single rose for ones beloved.

The soulless eyes of the demon question me,
Study me,
They beckon to me to come,
And sleep in their mistress Lilith's arms
The eyes promise me many things,
My eternal shadows that shroud my soul,
My soulless eyed demon within me.
Perhaps I will join it,
I know it will bring all my loves and my desires.
Demons and shadows are what make me who I am.

Queen of the Damned

Valencia Vaughn

It was a pleasure to submit.

It was pleasure to know that someone had a vested interest in me, my body, and my health. It was why I slipped on the red dress, covered my eyes, and waited for the camera to click.

A month earlier I had watched my daughter, a bloody mass of cells, fall out of me and into my hands as I crouched on cold wet tiles. At the time I didn't quite get what was happening; I only knew I was under a lot of stress. Approximately a month before that, the man I had fallen in love with had left me without even a goodbye. That same week, my Uncle passed, China died in the hospital, and the anniversary of my fiance's overdose took place. My body was weak and my headspace fragile to say the least. In about one month's time I lost her, my little baby, without even knowing she was with me.

I hated him for it, the father I mean. I hated him because I still loved him, and he didn't love me. I hated him because I secretly blamed him for her death. And in that moment of absolute desperation, Lilith stepped in. I was surprised by her presence. She embraced me, enveloped me, and showed me a side of her I had never seen before. She was the absolute Mother.

Weeks earlier, a Mexican Belly dancer had given me a red silk dress. The fabric clung to my body, accentuating the curves. Although the bloating from the pregnancy had gone down, my body still felt as if it was preparing for a child. I could feel every ache and muscle movement, none of this comparable to the emotional pain I felt on a daily basis. The dress itself made me feel slightly more human.

I don't connect to Deity the way most do. A specific time set aside for conversation does not work for me. It comes in waves, almost like a radio station with a bad signal. Most of my connection comes through art or music, and the way Lilith was communicating was through both. I knew in submitting to her I would have to do it publicly. I tilted my head back, lifted the head of the plastic snake, and let the camera work its magic. And with that one photograph, I had let her in, giving her my anger, my pain, and my fear. As the days went on, each photograph brought a different side of her.

I took them over a period of two weeks, and each time the camera flashed, clicked, and captured the image, I could feel her growing stronger within me. At first she came as anger. I would cry at the drop of a hat, even in the most inappropriate places. I wanted to scream and break glass bottles, but I knew it was what I needed. I gave my anger to Lilith; I gave her my blood and my trust, and in turn she took care of me, nurtured me, and told me her story.

The Mother:

From, dirt, blood, lust, and bone, her children were born. These demon children birthed at first were to make her former lover angry. But as each child came, she loved them more and more. In them she saw herself, and in them her legacy was imprinted. When Yahweh found out, he was furious. How dare this wretched woman disrespect his name? Yahweh had banished Lilith after she refused to lay under Adam. How could she? After being Yahweh's lover, how could she lay under this weak mortal? She refused his advances, and he, feeling jilted, went to Yahweh to complain. Yahweh showed no pity for his former lover as he banished her to the caves, and she, feeling hurt and disrespected, found solace in the company of the demons residing there. The demons regarded her as their Queen and did much to please her. And with these amorous entwines, she became pregnant and started to birth her many children. Yahweh retaliated with death. As fast as the children came, he attacked the babies and killed them.

Lilith was infuriated. These were her children, made from her flesh and bone. How could Yahweh, whom she loved so dearly, be so cruel? Her pain ran deep and her instinct to protect her offspring surged within her. She retaliated, and for every child of hers that was murdered, she would take a Jewish child in return. This became a war between them; for Yahweh it was a war of power and for Lilith, justice.

It's hard to describe the feeling a mother has for her children or even her unborn children. It's a protective warmth that flows through your chest and over your heart. It's an intense love that runs through you, a feeling that you would sacrifice anything to make this being happy and that you would die to protect them. And this I felt when I finally knew about my daughter. This was something Lilith and I shared. I felt safe with her, and she knew I had felt everything she had. She knew I had tasted the bitterness of unrequited love, the sadness of having a child die, and the anger of being disrespected. Lilith and I knew each other's paths very well. She took me in, and in return I gave her full reign over my body.

Months later I would find out more to this story. My daughter's father had demon blood. The amounts were trace, but somewhere down the line one of his family members crossed paths with a demon and the blood was introduced into his. It was hard for me to believe when I heard it and hard to grasp even now. Lilith had chosen him long ago, before we had met even, and our souls made a pact. I would become pregnant with a child that would be a direct line to her, and he would father it. He had two purposes in the agreement: 1. To be the father. 2. To take care of himself, as his path was hard. If he could come through on both of these things, his life would be fruitful and he would be given what he desired. If he failed, the punishment would be in Lilith's hands.

Unfortunately he did not come through on his end of the bargain. With the stress of what was going on around me, my body was weak, I was hurting, and Lilith had to take the child away. Her anger was deep; she was as much a part of her as she was mine. I knew there was nothing else I could do. She spoke bitterly. "I want him to know the pain we went through." She spoke for us but also of the agony of her relationship with Yahweh. It was out of my hands. All I could do was take care of myself and nurture my new spirit child. It still hurts, but as I move forward, my love for Lilith knows no bounds, and my empathy and trust in her runs deeper than any other blood bond I've known.

Lilith's Service

Raven Orthaevelve

I may as well tell you all up front that this essay is not from a normal perspective. I have been a sanguinarian vampire since Awakened in 1992, and I approach my religion and magic from a perspective that takes that into account. As such, the deities I worship have always been dark, and have included Hecate, Naga Kanya, Itzpapalotl, Tlatzolteotl, Artemis, the Morrigan, Sekhmet and Bastet, Oya, Tiamat and Kali. These deities have always been accepting of my nature, but it was Lilith who truly made me feel the most welcome and beloved.

I have been worshipping pagan deities for a long time, but it took me until less than five years ago to realize that most of the forms of the dark goddess that I had been revering were versions of the spirit of Lilith in various forms depending on culture. From another perspective, perhaps these other dark goddesses are more like her sisters or cousins if you do not believe in deities having different aspects. Looking back though, it has always been her I have spoken to, though in different forms.

Historical perspectives on Lilith have been addressed elsewhere in this book. To me, She is the mother of trees, the queen of all of beasts, the protector of outcasts, freaks and renegades and the adopted mother of outcasts of any kind. As such, she takes in those who fall through the cracks of society or just do not fit in. The homeless are under her protection, and so are those who are Gay,

Lesbian, Intersex or Transgender, as are those who are sex workers of any kind, and so are the darker types of Otherkin, such as vampires, Therians, Dark Fae and Dark elves or the Fallen.

Viola Johnson writes extensively on an interesting interpretation that is an oral tradition in her line of Sanguinarian vampires which was published before *Revelations of the Dark Mother*, which also alludes to the Cain/Lilith vampire mythos in her book *Dhampir: Child of the Blood*. While the book is old, it inspired a number of traditions still present in the modern Sanguinarian vampire community. Vi Johnson is also a long time member of the BDSM/Leather community in good standing, and I have wondered if Lilith inspired her involvement there though I have not had any opportunity to ask. Lilith is also mentioned in this oral tradition as being associated with shapeshifters as well as vampires, and at least one of my contacts has also mentioned that she is a patron of Therians and shapeshifters, espectially cat, owl, snake and wolf shifters. In my experience she enjoys it when I spend time with Therians or shifters as well as the darker Otherkin types.

As a part of the roleplaying game "Vampire: The Masquerade," a series of miniature books were published about the myth cycle of Cain and Lilith that was adapted for use in game canon. One of these books is called *Revelations of the Dark Mother*. While it is fictional, and the more hazardous practices in the book are NOT recommended, the feel of the book and the poetry within it is very true to Lilith's nature. I have used sections from this book as prayers or for meditation and had very good results.

As a priest in her tradition, it falls to me and those others who choose to work with her to represent her and act on her behalf and to bring honor to her name. This means seeking out those who consider themselves or who are outcasts and assisting them to an extent, while still allowing them to make their own decisions and mistakes. I may not interfere if someone chooses to ignore my advice and refuse my help, as that is and will always be their choice. There are no forcible interventions in my tradition, only the offer of help if it is wanted. My help can be connecting a person with organizations that help with financial aid or health care, teaching in various subjects, a spell or ritual on someone's behalf, certain forms of healing or, most often, simply talking with a person for hours until they feel some relief from whatever burdens they are carrying and perhaps a divination on their behalf.

I also do volunteer work as a phlebotomist at a local STD clinic as a form of service to Lilith. Many of the clients are sex workers, transgendered, gay, bisexual or queer individuals and the very poor, but we get people from all walks of life. In this way, I can aid those who Lilith holds dear and actually get my hands dirty instead of walling myself off from life's harshness as certain members of other faiths choose to do. It also constantly tests my self control as a vampire and my self discipline and compassion as well. This is very important to Lilith in my communications with her. She tends to choose survivors who are both compassionate and cruelly practical in a harmonious balance with each other.

My own introduction to darker deities came, as I have said, with my Awakening as a vampire. I had been working with some lighter deities, but I felt more and more that they disapproved of my nature and were drawing away from me, or perhaps it was the other way around. So I started researching the less bright and sparkly goddesses and found more of what I was looking for with them. Instead of gently holding you and asking if you wanted to do things differently next time, a dark Goddess will get your attention by whacking you with the psychic equivalent with a two by four, then showing you and telling you loudly exactly why and how you screwed up and demanding that you fix it. If you don't, in my experience, they do not punish you. They just withdraw and wait for your own bad decision to come back and bite you in the sensitive parts, allow you to apologize for not taking good advice and insist that you learn from your mistake instead of repeating it.

Lilith is one of these and demands that her followers be survivors, physically and mentally tough. Her priests and lay worshipers must show self-discipline, courage and initiative and not be sexually prudish or judgmental. In certain cases Lilith has asked that I, as her priestess, use sacred sex as a healing technique for others, or that I consider being intimate with someone she admires or respects in her stead. I always have the freedom to refuse these requests, but so far I have never wanted to. She and I have much the same taste in lovers. On occasion she has also showed me how to feed vampirically off someone and draw out pain, illness or other energies through their blood, and then give them to Lilith to dispose of. Again, I have the right to refuse, but I have never wanted to. She will occasionally possess me during sex with a man she has taken a particular liking to. This experience always leaves me with memories that are not mine of intimacy at night in a desert, feeling my wings extended and talons for fingernails, and leaves me with a rush of energy afterward. At other times she will occasionally talk to someone for hours using my mouth to convey messages. I never remember what is said during these talks, as the words are not meant for me and the sense of spiritual ecstasy afterward usually has me walking around with tons of energy and a goofy grin on my face.

I have encountered her in my dreaming journeys in a small stone courtyard with a stone pool full of black liquid at the center. The courtyard seems to be suspended in space, with stars all around it and above and below. This is dizzying and terrifying until you get used to it. She usually is waiting for me there, and seems to have a chitinous armor coating of shiny jet black when I meet her in this place over all of her body save for her wings, bird feet, neck and head. I have never read anyone else seeing this form of armor on her, so I can only imagine it is associated with my following a Warrior path as well as a priestly one. The other location I see her in the astral plane is a ring of standing stones in an ancient forest. The moon is always full there and the trees are stirred by a constant breeze. There she wears dyed black deerskin clothes reminiscent of the buckskin clothing of a Woodland Native American tribe, but with no beadwork or decoration and no moccasins. She always has the talons of a bird for feet and iridescent black wings, and her beauty is dazzling. I feel she wears clothes or armor because the few times she has appeared naked, her beauty and sensuality dazzled me so much that I could do very little besides stammer, stare and try not to lust after her while she was trying to instruct me.

Lilith also enjoys offerings of sex without the desire for procreation and the offerings of the sexual fluids that result. She also favors BDSM and its practice, and very much enjoys the offering of disposables from such activity such as plastic handcuffs, needles, razors, used rubbing alcohol wipes and the like. Tattoo bandages are also a good offering as they represent a form of chosen ordeal that permanently changes you and makes you stand out from those around her. She is not a deity to invoke if you are seeking a lifetime or permanent partner, as she does not enjoy monogamy in my experience. As her priestess and adopted child, I do not take part in or attend marriages, as every time I have done so, the marriage has dissolved within two years time or less. This may be different for other followers of hers. She also, in my experience, favors those who adopt children to those who have them, and very much favors those who adopt rescued animals of all kinds.

In my tradition, her priests choose to give up things in their lives as offerings to her, such as brightly colored clothing, the use of alcohol or recreational drugs and certain foods. However, she is a practical goddess, and if it is a choice between eating a food I have chosen to give up or going hungry, she will encourage me to go ahead and eat! The same is true with clothing; if I must wear a piece of clothing for a job as a uniform, it is permitted. At home and off duty though, I dress in black, grey, navy blue, brown and dark green. Jewelry is permitted to me, as I am a jeweler and she is the inspiration behind many of my pieces. I shave the sides of my head to show that I follow a protector path and as another offering to her. On occasion she has asked that I dye my hair half dark red and half black, and I have complied. She has never asked me to do anything that would violate my honor or my conscience, and I cannot imagine that she would ever want blind obedience. A huge part of her essence is not only self-discipline to make indulged pleasures so much the sweeter, but the freedom of choice in all things.

Of all the gods I have worked with, only she has helped me to finally get what I wanted most in life. For that I will be forever grateful. I hear others talk about struggling to hear or understand their gods, but I have never had that problem with her. She has always been willing to talk to me, though she never tells me what to do at tough decision points in my life. Even if I make a mistake, she is there to help me through it in her own way. Her path is one of pain with meaning and the attempt to understand what life's lessons have to teach. Every painful experience is a lesson, a chance to learn the hard way so you do not have to repeat the lesson or the pain.

To be Lilith's priest is first to learn to survive, then to thrive in places most people would never go, socially and physically. Each person who dedicates himself to her is a piece of iron ore in her hands. She will melt, smelt, purify, hammer, quench, sharpen and etch that ore as she needs to in order to make her dedicant a worthy tool in her hands. In the end, the dedicant has been transformed and can never go back to who or what they were before. Working with Lilith changes you permanently. It changed me from a suburban Yuppie brat to a self-sufficient, fiercely independent person who cannot respect those who do not stand up for and truly understand themselves.

For offerings, Lilith tends to enjoy any of the items below, as well as bits of cloth with menstrual blood burned outside for her, cornmeal, scraps of silk, hand made powdered incense, apple cider and cranberry juice libations, and anything made by hand by her worshipers in her honor. She has no problem sharing an altar with other gods or spirits but absolutely detests the Ancient Egyptian god Set due to his mistreatment of his wife Nephythis in mythology. Be warned, do not invoke them in the same ritual or place their statues on the same altar!

If you wish to invite her into your life, consider planting a garden, or setting up a terrarium or aquarium and making tiny (a drop or two) offerings of your own blood (or women can offer menstrual blood). This is a sort of personal world to teach you that you must nurture and weed dispassionately with the same hand. It can teach you how your actions affect your worlds, both inner and outer. It also allows you to bring a small portion of Lilith's wilderness home indoors. Tarragon is her special plant, but she also likes Roses, nightshade, Greenbriar, wormwood, yew, vervain, mandrake, may apple, plum, pomegranate, yarrow, tulip, thyme, fungus, moss, cypress and other plants that have her energy. A fountain indoors with plants or a window box for those with little space are also appropriate, as long as you can show the beauty of wildness and the need for careful stewardship and the occasional bit of dispassionate weeding and pruning. The self-discipline necessary for such a garden also pleases her. Carved and tumbled gems please her as well, especially amethyst, black pearl, onyx, mahogany obsidian, apache tear, smokey quartz, amber, shell, jet, black tourmaline, blue sheen obsidian, red jasper, carnelian, bloodstone, bone, ruby, dark blue or black sapphire, star diopside (a personal favorite stone) magnetite, hematite and apatite.

Queen of Knowledge: Lilith the Teacher

A Knife in the Dark

Christina Lythia H.

When I was thirteen, I was spiritually lost and confused. I was heading down a road of self-destruction, and I didn't care who I brought with me. I was on the internet just browsing different sites when I stumbled upon one about paganism.

I felt drawn to a page talking of dark goddesses, and the first name I noticed on the list was Lilith.

Something inside me chimed. I felt compelled to research her, to learn more about her. Something inside of me came alive. When I said her name, my spirit felt whole.

Anyone who has found their spiritual path knows what I mean when you feel complete. A part of you changes, and a hole that nothing seemed to fill suddenly is healed.

When I would think about Lilith, my heart felt good, and I was happy. I was sure then that I would have her as my guide and Goddess. Some weeks later I had a dream.

I was in my room, in my bed and something caught my eye. It was a doll, pale, black hair and at first I was afraid when it looked at me. It smiled and its eyes glowed as it started to speak.

The doll said, "My name is Lilith, prove you love me!" I found a knife beside me and stabbed the doll. I felt a presence and then the doll disappeared.

I know some people will say that Lilith is no Goddess to be

worshiped, she is not real, or why would you want to worship and revere a child-killing, man-seducing demon?

But anyone who believes in a God, Goddess or both know that what they believe is real and that all beings have faults, and sometimes those beings aren't as bad as they are made out to be.

Lilith has blessed me in many ways, making my life better than it ever has been. I can't imagine not being devoted to her for all she has done for me. So yes, she might be a blood-sucking, child-killing demoness in history and writings, but she's my Goddess, and I know that she will protect and comfort me from now until eternity.

Besides, everyone deserves a second chance when they have a crummy reputation.

Creatrix, Undertow

Kirsten Brown

She likes silver and pomegranate wine and bourbon, strong coffee, chili peppers and darkest chocolate, myrrh and dragon's blood. Her kind of deep, tidal magic pushes hardest at the dark moon, during lunar eclipses, or when I'm bleeding. The thing she is known most and best for is only the barest beginning of the facets I've seen of her. She has come to me as mother, teacher, sister and lover. As Eve's dark twin with razored teeth between her legs, leading strange hounds, Giger's biomechanical siren in the Shells of the Sephiroth, Leviathan in the cold, dark depths of time, or the voices of the owls that live behind my house and in my garden. She is a dark mirror to Lucifer's illumination and black, still waters to Babalon's fire, the discerning darkness that keeps secrets from all but the most determined, and the void that all light is lost in, no matter how brilliant. When one approaches Lilith, they must ignite and carry their own light.

I've been dragging these words out ever so slowly, and wondering how it is that I could have nothing to say about a deity who has been here with me, part of me, for nearly half of my life. Who has been a crucial part of me defining who I am as it finally dawns on me that I am a woman, not a girl. At the same time, I know it is not that I have nothing to say, but rather that it is hard to put any of it into words, simply because the connection is a part of me. Try describing what it is like to have arms or legs or breasts to someone who never did. I wrote this because of her. I was ridden to, because I often have a hard time believing in the things I create, and their worth.

Working with Lilith has been difficult, at times uncomfortable. She is always closest when I am pushing myself or my boundaries, whether they are mental, physical or something else, the voice that whispers, "*more, this is not enough, you are better than any scars you may get from this, or will be when you are through.*" She is that which showed me anger, taught me the laser focus and giddying madness of it, showed me the self that would cheerfully lick my own wounds, metaphoric or no, and go back for more. I then had to learn on my own that this wasn't always a helpful tactic. Though I had done my own, tamer rite years ago, her initiation came over three insomniac nights spread over some months, in downright pornographic visions, half-dreams somewhere between waking and sleep that were deeply uncomfortable for someone only just beginning to own their bi nature. In one of these, I lost my ring finger to her and was given a new one, clawed and reptilian. Working through her sphere of the Qliphoth (a journey I still haven't finished) I have found myself hunting down, killing, and taking trophies from monstrous versions of myself, all the terrible and detrimental self-images I've accumulated over the years.

It is not worship, because she does not want someone who kneels that way; it is a lessoning, an overcoming, a thrashing me into shape. She wants strength in her children, and will achieve it harshly if need be. Her connections have influenced other facets of my practice, pushed me in other directions I wouldn't have found otherwise, but she has always been one of the pillars, something that was always beneath it all, and the primary female figure of my practice. Until fairly recently, she was the only Goddess I worked with alongside various Gods, because I've never quite gotten along with other women.

There are a myriad things that Lilith embodies that females have been accused of and abused for, for centuries. Baneful magics, shrieking, bringing storms. Being a bitch, born corrupt, lustful, shameless. Mothering monsters. I am not certain that any of these things are inherently bad, unless you take them as bad. 'Bitch' is often a blanket term for a woman who sets her boundaries clearly and unarguably, 'slut' and 'shameless' for one who has owned their sex and drives, and 'witch', for a woman who is cunning and creative and does not take lightly to being made a doormat. I'd say all of these things are things to strive towards, not to fear.

As for being a mother of demons and monsters, this can be taken as a pejorative, or it can become another way of looking at her; not just as the Dark Mother archetype, but a Muse and a catalyst as well, a thing of evolution and iteration. Myth has long tried to make women into something Other, and the Other into something frightening and terrible by its nature, but being different is only terrible if you fear the unknown. As an artist as well as a magician, to me she *is* the transformation and change implied by that Otherness. Becoming it, understanding the strangeness and shadows and dark parts of the self by taking it all in and creating with it. Not just accepting, but inviting the Other into your bed and your Self, becoming or bringing into being something more than what you began with through that intimate exposure. Throwing yourself into your magic and taking it all in, however you enact it, and going from one who 'does' to one who 'is'.

She is the bridge between the antinomian, the human, and the empyrean, pushing us to be more than primate programming by taking control of and weaponising fear. Lilith began, according to myth, as a woman, and through sheer Will and what she chose to allow within her, sloughed this off like skin to become a great demon, a force of nature armed with the names of God, and a Goddess in her own right.

Lilith: A Personal Reflection

Marcus

I started investigating Lilith in 2001 with my search into other belief systems. Much of my life had been spent in Christian schools, so I decided to see what else was out there. My first stop away from my previous path was to study about the Wiccan religion. However, I never considered myself Wiccan nor do I now. While I recognize the wisdom behind the Wiccan religion, I feel compelled to follow the road that Lilith has chosen for me. I seek to honor her in all of the forms I have come to know, and I have known quite a few of them. She is my Goddess, mother, protector, mentor, and savior.

Lilith rescued me from my seemingly endless despair in 2004. She taught me that life really was worth living. Instead of despair, she instilled in me a hunger for life. With her help, I was able to learn about other beings that have come to me one by one to introduce themselves according to their own terms. Sometimes they come by whispers in the wind, a visualization, a dream, or symbols left for me like bread crumbs leading me on a quest to find hidden messages. There are also occasions when they chose to come through the voices of those closest to me.

Lilith is an eternal flame within me. I can feel her in my veins and taste her fiery disposition on my lips. She fills my mind, body, and spirit with feelings of supreme bliss. When she calls me to her mirror, I am consumed with sensations of complete rapture.

Without hesitation, she shows me the deeper areas of myself. One way I get answers from her is by drawing a pentagram on a mirror. Afterward, I gaze into the center with a question in mind. Of course, she gives me an answer on her own terms and when it is her desire to do so. In my experience, she does not respond well to being rushed. In addition, she neither speaks to the ego nor coddles it. Rather, she embraces the art of taking responsibility for one's own actions. While not without mercy, she neither gives pity to those who feel sorry for themselves nor does she fix one's problems. In short, I have found that she is not a being that one runs to in order to make everything all better. However, she will give excellent advice to those who seek to help themselves.

In 2006, Lilith chose to reward me by allowing me to find my twin flame. Like my visions of Lilith, she has red hair and green eyes with the same fiery disposition Lilith permitted me to taste so many times before. Now I think of my twin flame as my Goddess as well. I tend to embrace a feministic view of Lilith in that I quite often feel Lilith gave me to my twin flame as a present. Both Lilith and she inspire a lot of devotion in me. Without a doubt, I desire to please them both.

To me, Lilith is the spice of life. She is the essence of fire and the power in the wind. In her embrace, I feel the strength to take responsibility for my own happiness, to embrace the blessings of freedom, and feel the joys of individuality. I proudly wear her mark upon my mind and spirit. Perhaps one day I will also wear her mark upon my body. I would only mark my body for her and my twin flame. It would be my gift and my ordeal. Lilith would appreciate such a gift because she is the one of the forces who called me to the ordeal path. My twin flame would appreciate such a gift because she knows it would be a token of my love for her, one that I would not take lightly.

Another key aspect of Lilith that I have come to love is her role as my instructor in the arts of the feminine mysteries. She has shown me the power of the female body to not only give life but to act as a gateway to the divine essences of the cosmos. Moreover, she has dispelled any negativity toward menstruation I might have possessed before by illustrating its power rather than shunning it as a curse. Menstruation is a very beautiful and very powerful process by which women can harness unimaginable power and creativity. It is a time when women are extremely potent in their magical abilities. Lilith has called my attention to the power of menstrual blood and a woman's moon. She has infused me with reverence for the female body and its capabilities. Women have the ability to harness the power of the maiden, mother, and crone. They hold within them the keys to life, death, and rebirth. I thank Lilith for showing me that, and I thank my twin flame for embracing her inner Goddess.

When I need to get in the mood to write, I can count on my twin flame to be my inspiration. She is, indeed, my other half. Mother Lilith gave me the greatest gift she could have in this world when she allowed me to meet the one who completes me in every way. Many nights I cried myself to sleep as my entire being craved to be with the one I felt so strongly within me. Before I met my twin flame, I felt her calling to me. With Lilith's help, I was able to not only find out where the voice was coming from but follow it to meet the one in my thoughts, the one in my dreams. It has not been an easy relationship and has presented many challenges. While it has not been easy, it has been rewarding. Anything worthwhile takes time, work, and dedication. Lilith has taught me to be patient as I reveal my inner tool box. According to Lilith, I already had everything I would ever need to succeed within myself. All I had to do was realize it and be prepared to use the tools I already possessed. Yes, Lilith could have simply given me everything, but it would not have the same flavor that it has now. It would not mean as much. Hard work and dedication are what give the fruits of labor their sweetness.

Over time, Lilith has found numerous ways to harness my anger, tears, and frustration into a creatively productive force. She has explained to me that emotion is like water and can be used much like hydropower. Anger, tears, and frustration are emotional responses that involve a lot of energy that can be collected through writing. It is through writing that I have learned to control my anger, to collect my tears and transmute them into words on a page, and to ease my frustration by composing something truly valuable. Writing can also be used to communicate with other beings. Automatic writing is another tool I use to converse with Lilith. When I channel Lilith, I feel an infusion of refreshing energy, and I can feel that energy forming into words. When I read those words on a page, I feel comforted, and I have the knowledge that I can succeed in my endeavors.

Lady of Answers

You are the lady of answers
Who comes in the form of soothing whispers.
I know you care even though you make
Me wait for what I crave and desire to take.
You force me to be patient for my own sake
As you caution me to beware of the embers
Within so I do not burnout and fall prey to the rake.
Fire needs air to burn and in time the flames can rise
Higher and higher into the sky if one is truly wise
And allows the air to caress the flames.

Lilith is the Dark Shekinah, a dweller that I invite within my being to aid me in my quest to achieve gnosis, spiritual knowledge. Through her, I am empowered to not only know but put my knowledge into action. She allows me to stand open Malkuth and make my way through the Tree of Life to the Kether. If I wish to peer into the depths of Daat, she offers encouragement with a liberal dose of warning that I not allow myself to be completely pulled away from my senses as I gaze into the mouth of the abyss. As I listen to the abysmal whispers, I question everything I have previously been taught. At the beckoning of the whispers, I am reborn and find myself in Lilith's arms. When I look into her eyes, I no longer miss the part of me that was transformed by her dark light. Within her dark embrace, I feel androgynous and very much a part of her as she embodies the Dark Shakti and kills my ego much like Kali. While under the essence of Lilith, I can feel my kundalini rising. She and her consort Samael become twin serpents united under the being known as Baphomet, and I fall into a realm of pleasure comparable only to that with my twin flame.

Finally, I would like to describe my relationship with Lilith in terms of Spiritual BDSM. Lilith is the epitome of female domination. While I have found that she detests the concept of slavery, she does not mind sexual dominance and submission. In fact, she can be quite playful whether invoked or evoked. However, she can also be stern and does not respond well to disobedience. When she gives a command, she fully expects it to be obeyed. Otherwise, she can be quite creative in her attempts to secure obedience. It is for that reason I am drawn to her method of BDSM. She does not hold back, accept excuses, or apologize. From her, I learned that Spiritual BDSM involves sacrifice and surrender. Moreover, she drove home the point that it was a way of life. Through Lilith, I learned to be of service to the Dark Goddess in all of he forms. She introduced me to other Dark Goddesses such as Ereskigal, Hecate, Hela, Kali, Persephone, Nyx and the Morrigan. Demetra George and Raven Kaldera are two writers who have profoundly influenced me in my path to serve the Dark Goddess. Demetra George's *Mysteries of the Dark Moon: The Healing Power of the Dark Goddess* and Raven Kaldera's *Dark Moon Rising: Pagan BDSM and the Ordeal Path* are two books that I would highly recommend to those who would like to delve deeper into the above concepts. Demetra George's book helped me to understand my feelings, and Raven Kaldera's book helped me to apply those feelings to BDSM.

It seems so long ago since that night in 2004 when Lilith came to rescue me from my depression. She has come to mean so many things to me. I could shower her with countless titles and thank her for what she has done for me until the end of time, but it will not be sufficient. I cannot fully express what she means to me. If I wrote a book of poetry to her with my own blood and bound it with my own flesh, I could not give her enough of myself. Everyday she teaches me to be thankful for each breath I take and each heartbeat my heat is permitted to make.

Transformed by Her Will

Lillith ThreeFeathers Lewis

To some, Lilith is a maiden, blithely tripping through the forest
on a perfect spring morning surrounded by her animal companions
— but not to me. When I see Her, She stands tall and strong.
Muscles etch Her body and Her hair swirls in the breeze, moving
the air, creating the storm, taming the wind. She is virginal in the
oldest sense of the word, that is, absolutely complete, an
incomprehensible and acknowledged totality.

The year I met Lilith was emotionally and physically a roller
coaster ride. It was the kind of year that others, those who did not
have to live through it, would describe as "challenging" and
"transitional." Such intellectualized words did not match reality.
Exhausted and ill,I was struggling to raise my children alone. Then,
the other shoe dropped. The confident high-priced specialists
agreed: at best, I would live another three years.

Medicine had run out of answers, but I was not ready to give up
— and I wanted to survive. I needed to raise my children, to see
them grow into adulthood. Not knowing where to turn, I raised my
voice to the stars and to the moon shining in the night. At that
moment, bowed under the weight of my soul's sorrow, I called for
something — anything — to change my life, regardless of the cost.

At first I did not recognize the answer. Night after night, I
awakened to mists drifting through the closed window into my
bedroom. On the dark moon, I heard a rhythmical tapping on the

glass pane. At last dragging myself from my bed, I went to investigate. There, on my windowsill, stood an owl. Amazed I stared, my mind blank and numb.

The next night, She walked into my room and quietly waited for me to notice. "Beautiful" barely described Her face. Her long hair stirred and then stilled. leather jerkin. Soft white cloth floated around her legs, melting and reforming as if dancing.

Decisively, She acted. She set my feet on the crags — dragging me from the established nest of my existence. Her whirlwind scattered my life and blew the tatters of this reality to another place. In an instant, I found myself running with the wild beasts in the midst of a flaming wood. As the owl flew silently over head, She led me down a dim path. While the forest crackled behind me, strange sounds erupted from the trees to either side. And still I dashed behind Her.

In the morning, I awakened tangled in drenched sheets. The following night, She appeared again. And again, the next.

Who was this goddess laying claim to me? I asked, "Who are you?"

"Lilith," was the response that enfolded me. At that time, I had no idea who She was. Although I did not know it, the balance of my life had been shifted. Through the months, my nights were filled with healings, ceremonies, shadows and whispers that I dimly remembered when awake. Her transformation took the form of the snake, not the butterfly. Her touch induced the labor pains of revolution as conversion and zeal impelled me onwards. Half-blinded by the scrap of my skin on the rock of conventionality and habit, I fought my way back to life. Feverishly gasping, I emerged stripped of certainty, scoured of my habits — clean.

Through all of this, those around me shook their heads at my folly. Those who had known me for years offered consistent opinions. "You're doing what? Tai Chi? Shamanism? What is wrong with you? You've gotten so weird. Why don't you just find a nice man? You really need to settle down." While they gossiped about me, clucking their tongues at my alteration, I discovered that I did not really mind their judgments nor their misunderstandings.

For Her blood heated mine and Her breath invigorated my days. Through Her, I discovered new sensations and strange ideas that brought a subtle calmness. No longer could I passively feel the sun's rays. Now, I basked in them, feeling the furnace settle into my heart. No longer did the moon feel cold and distant because moonbeams now lodged in my head.

Yet, still She was not done with me.

One day my 12-year old son and his uncle walked to the nearby river to go fishing. A bit of time passed and then frantic pounding on the door. "He didn't listen to me. He fell. I can't reach him. I think he's hurt." Two years previously, I could not walk a block without stopping four times to catch my breath, but now, without thought, I began to run side-by-side with him. Was She running with me or for me? I don't know. In fact, I don't remember much about that dash down the hill to the river. Yet, in the next moment,

I stood on the riverbank, desperately reaching to pluck my child to safety and carry him up the rocks away from the water.

In that instinctive moment of rescue, I saved not only my son but also myself.

And there I stood, at the top of the riverbank—panting and tired, yes—but I held my son safe in my arms. Turning back towards the river, still holding him tightly, I looked down the steep rocky slope. And then, I realized what I had done—what She had accomplished.

Through all of those months of physical and spiritual work, pushing and pulling, She had propelled me towards the future. Perhaps from Her place in the universe, Her actions were simple logic; maybe She knew She was prodding me to this very moment when I would yank my son from the stony river. True awareness grew: She had resuscitated me. Not only had She brought me back from illness and returned my life, She had given me the power to reach my son and carry him to safety. Persistently, lovingly, She had rocked my world, and nothing could ever be the same. Standing there, silently clutching my son, I gave thanks to Her.

Twenty years have passed, and my son is grown and married. Even now, Lilith shines in my life like a star emerging in the night sky. Look, do you see Her? I catch a glimpse of Her gleaming from behind a moving wisp of cloudbank. Again She comes, striding into the room on mist and moonbeams. Just over there. She waits for you.

Thus have I seen Her.

Epilogue: In Her Words

(transcribed March 20, 2009 by Anya Kless)

Remember that you have your own power. You are not merely a lackey. You are not just a lump of clay to be molded. You have your own power within you that they cannot touch. Your power is innate and of the body. It is all you know without knowing.

It is easy to give up all power. It is harder to retain ownership, hard to negotiate. You are a negotiator—negotiate. Ask. You must have something going for you if everyone wants a piece. You are not a victim to the slaughter. Never fall into that role—it is false.

Your power is a stick of dynamite. Destruction. Creation. Power. Fire. Rebellion. Worthy of attention.

I am the snake—poison and transformation. Movement. Learn from me. Be me.

You are a priest within a sanctuary. Create your sanctuary to feel your power.

You are a vessel and a seat of power. Open to your own power.

Further Reading

These sources approach Lilith with varying agendas, opinions, and levels of scholarly accuracy. I do not endorse or agree with everything they say about Lilith. You probably won't either. Read with discernment, have a good debate or two, and enjoy.

In Print:

The Book of Jewish Symbols. Ed. Ellen Frankel and Betsy Franklin Teutcsh. Northvale, NJ: Jason Aronson Inc., 1992.

M. Kelley Hunter. *Living Lilith: Four Dimensions of the Cosmic Feminine.* Bournemouth, UK: The Wessex Astrologer Ltd, 2009.

Hurwitz, Siegmund. *Lilith—The First Eve, Historical and Psychological Aspects of the Dark Feminine.* (1980) Trans. Gela Jacobson. Revised Second Edition. Einsiedeln, Switzerland: DaimonVerlag, 1999.

Kaldera, Raven. *Hermaphrodeities: The Transgender Spirituality Workbook.* Second Edition. Hubbardston, MA: Asphodel Press, 2008.

Koltuv, Barbara Black. *The Book of Lilith.* York Beach, ME: Nicolas-Hays, 1986.

Patai, Raphael. *The Hebrew Goddess.* (1967) Third Enlarged Edition. Detroit: Wayne State University Press, 1990.

Schwartz, Howard. *Lilith's Cave: Jewish Tales of the Supernatural.* New York: Oxford University Press, 1988.

Sullivan, Tammy. *Pagan Anger Magic: Positive Transformations from Negative Energies.* New York: Citadel Press, 2005.

Online:

The Lilith Shrine: http://www.lilitu.com/lilith

The Jewish Pagan Resource Page: http://www.lilitu.com/jap

The Lilith Institute: http://www.lilithinstitute.com

Jewish/Christian Literature Resources on Lilith:
http://jewishchristianlit.com//Topics/Lilith/index.html

Lilith Magazine: http://www.lilith.org

The Lilith Library: http://www.lilithgallery.com/library/index.html

43005477R00079